ANCIENT CO[...]
THE HISTORIC C[...]
OF RURAL D[...]

A report on the
Devon Historic Landscape Characterisation Project

D910

SAM TURNER

DEVON ARCHAEOLOGICAL SOCIETY OCCASIONAL PAPER 20

First published in 2007 by the Devon Archaeological Society
c/o Royal Albert Memorial Museum,
Queen Street, Exeter, EX4 3RX, UK
http://www.groups.ex.ac.uk/das/

ISBN 10: 0-9527899-8-1
ISBN 13: 978-0-9527899-8-7

British Library Cataloguing in Publication Data.

A catalogue record for this book is available from the British Library.

The Society is grateful to English Heritage for supporting the publication of this volume.

Printed for the Society by Short Run Press,
Bittern Road, Sowton, Exeter, Devon EX2 7LN

CONTENTS

For my mother, Helen,
who loves Devon

LIST OF ILLUSTRATIONS

ACKNOWLEDGEMENTS

I am grateful to all those involved in the Devon HLC project for their support and encouragement. Bill Horner has been a patient and helpful manager and adviser throughout. Graham Fairclough and Frances Griffith oversaw the project and provided innumerable insights. I had invaluable discussions with Brian Carpenter, Peter Child, Ann Dick, Martin Fletcher, Faye Glover, Debbie Griffiths, Sean Hawken, Peter Herring, Simon Probert, Anne Richards, Lucy Ryder, Tim Selman, and other members of the project's Advisory Committee. In preparing this book I have benefited from support and discussion with colleagues including Jim Crow, Jon Finch, Chris Fowler, Harold Fox, Kevin Greene, Mark Jackson, Naomi Standen and Tom Williamson. I am grateful to Eileen Standen for proofreading the text, to Jane Olorenshaw for preparing the index, to Sarah Lynch for redrawing figs 4, 100 and 110, and to Claudia Dürrwächter, Djamila Hassani and Morgane Quetel for translating the Summaries.

The Devon HLC project was funded and supported by English Heritage, Devon County Council, Dartmoor National Park Authority and Tamar Valley Area of Outstanding Natural Beauty (2001-4), and by English Heritage, Devon County Council and Newcastle University's School of Historical Studies (2004-6)).

I am grateful to *Antiquity* Publications Ltd, Cambridge University Press, Devon County Council and Devon Record Office, English Heritage, Chris Chapman (for more of his photographs, please see www.chrischapmanphotography.com), Getmapping plc, Frances Griffith, Bill Horner, Landmark Information Group Ltd, Rosemary Robinson and Simon Timms for their help and kind permission to use their photographs or other copyright images in this book.

Newcastle, June 2007

SUMMARY

Devon has a rich and fascinating rural landscape. This book provides an introduction to Devon's historic landscape and presents a new kind of landscape archaeology for the county, based on the results of the Devon Historic Landscape Characterisation (HLC) project (2001-5).

From prehistoric times to the present, every age has left distinctive traces that help shape today's landscape. The book shows how research into this historic landscape can help us understand better both the lives of our predecessors, and today's rural environment.

The first chapter of this book outlines the historic character of Britain's principal landscape regions, and how the historic landscape of Devon compares with other parts of England.

Chapter 2 gives an introduction to the development of Historic Landscape Characterisation, and describes the methodology adopted for the Devon HLC project. HLC is a method for mapping, presenting and understanding the landscape with reference to its historical development. HLC has a developing range of applications in landscape research, management and planning.

Most of lowland Devon is dominated by fields whose origins lie in the Middle Ages. Chapter 3 discusses the character of Devon's fields and their historical development.

A fundamental characteristic of the Devon landscape is that different landscape types are often found mixed together in complex patterns. Chapter 4 discusses the histories of some of the most important historic land-use types, including orchards, watermeadows, woodland and rough ground. Using the HLC can help us to map these variations and interrelationships in more detail than most other large-scale techniques.

As elsewhere in England, Devon's landscape can be divided into different regions or *pays*. Each of Devon's regions has a distinctive character, created over the centuries by particular combinations of farming, industry and other activities. Archaeological and historical research can unravel the historic patterns in the landscape to help us understand these histories. Chapter 5 investigates how the HLC data can help us to investigate and appreciate these patterns from the past.

Finally, Chapter 6 considers the future of Devon's historic rural landscape. It uses the HLC to illustrate some trajectories of change in the 20th century, in particular by focusing on vulnerable landscape types. It argues that the results of the HLC project could make a useful contribution to the conservation and enhancement of the rural landscape, and to debates on the preservation and reinforcement of local distinctiveness in the future.

RÉSUMÉ

La région du Devon est dotée d'un paysage riche et fascinant. Cet ouvrage offre une introduction au paysage historique du Devon et présente une nouvelle forme d'archéologie paysagiste du conté, basée sur les résultats émis par le projet Devon Historic Landscape Characterisation (HLC – la caractérisation du paysage historique), conduit de 2001 à 2005.

Les ères se succédant, de la préhistoire à nos jours, ont chacune laissé une trace distinctive contribuant à la formation du paysage actuel. Ce livre démontre comment l'étude de ce paysage historique peut nous permettre de mieux comprendre la vie de nos prédécesseurs, ainsi que l'environnement rural d'aujourd'hui.

Le premier chapitre propose un compte-rendu du caractère historique des principales régions Britanniques, et établit ensuite une comparaison entre le paysage historique du Devon et celui d'autres régions anglaises.

Le second chapitre est une introduction au développement de l'Historic Landscape Characterisation (HLC); il décrit la méthodologie appliquée par le projet Devon HLC. HLC est une méthode combinant la cartographie, la présentation et l'analyse du paysage en référence à son développement historique. HLC a développé une série de programmes pour la recherche sur le paysage, sa gestion et son aménagement.

La majeure partie de la basse terre du Devon est dominée par des champs dont les origines datent du Moyen Age. Le chapitre 3 se penche sur l'aspect de ces champs et leur développement historique. L'une des caractéristiques fondamentales du paysage du Devon est que différents types de paysages sont souvent entremêlés en schémas complexes. Le chapitre 4 s'intéresse aux genèses des types d'aménagements du territoire les plus importants, y incluant les vergers, les prés ou pairies inondables, les bois et les landes. L'utilisation de la méthode HLC nous permet de combiner ces variantes et ces interrelations de façon plus précise que la plupart des autres techniques de grande échelle.

Comme partout ailleurs en Angleterre, le paysage du Devon est divisible en pays. Chacune des pays du Devon a un caractère distinctif, créé au fil des siècles par une unique combinaison d'agriculture, d'industrie et d'autres activités. La recherche archéologique et historique permet de dénouer les schémas historiques dans la formation des paysages et nous aide ainsi à comprendre ces évolutions historiques. Le chapitre 5 étudie la manière dont la méthode de collection d'informations utilisée par le projet HLC peut nous aider à examiner et comprendre ces schémas du passé.

Enfin, le chapitre 6 prend en considération le futur du paysage historique rural du Devon. Sur la base de la méthode HLC, quelques changements ayant eu lieu au 20ème siècle sont présentés ; une attention particulière a été portée sur les paysages de type vulnérable. Ce chapitre démontre que les conclusions obtenues par le projet HLC pourraient apporter une contribution positive à la conservation et au développement des paysages ruraux ; ces résultats enrichiront également les débats sur la préservation et le renforcement de la particularité locale dans le futur.

Djamila Hassani
Morgane Quetel

ZUSAMMENFASSUNG

Die britische Grafschaft Devon zeichnet sich durch eine facettenreiche und aussergewöhnliche Landschaft aus. Dieses Buch gibt einen geschichtlichen Überblick in die Entwicklung dieser Landschaft und stellt einen neuen Zweig der Landschaftsarchäologie vor, der auf den Ergebnissen des 'Devon Historic Landscape Characterisation project' (HLC – Historische Landschaftscharakterisierung) basiert.

Jedes Zeitalter hinterlässt Spuren die sich bis heute in der Landschaft wiederfinden lassen. Dieses Buch zeigt auf, wie Studien zur Landschaftsentwicklung uns zu einem besseren Verständnis unserer Vorfahren führen können und zudem helfen die gegenwärtige Entwicklung ländlicher Gegenden besser zu verstehen.

Das erste Kapitel beschreibt die Hauptkarakteristiken der britischen Grafschaften und zeigt auf wie Devon sich im Verhältnis zu anderen Teilen Grossbritanniens historisch entwickelt hat.

Das zweite Kapitel gibt eine Einführung in die 'Historic Landscape Charaterisation' (HLC) und stellt die im Devon HLC Projekt verwendeten Methoden vor. HLC kann dazu verwendet werden, Landschaften unter Berücksichtigung ihrer historischen Entwicklung zu kartieren, abzubilden und zu verstehen. Dieses Verfahren findet zunehmend Anwendung in den Bereichen Landschaftsforschung, -managment und –planung.

Devon zeichnet sich dadurch aus, dass seine Region sich aus einer Mischung verschiedener Landschaftstypen zusammensetzt, die ein komplexes Muster ergeben. Kapitel 4 gibt einen Überblick über die wichtigsten Arten der Landschaftsnutzung, (inklusive Wiesen, Obstgarten und Waldland) und deren historische Entwicklung. HLC ermöglicht eine detailliertere Wiedergabe von Variationen und Zusammenhängen zwischen Landschaftnutzung als herkömmliche Techniken.

Die Grafschaft Devon kann, wie andere Teile Grossbritanniens, in verschiedene Regionen unterteilt werden. Jede dieser Regionen hat unverwechselbare Eigenschaften, die sich aus ihrer landwirtschaftlichen Nutzung in den letzten Jahrhunderten entwickelt haben. Archäologische und historische Quellen können uns dabei helfen, diese historisch gewachsenen Muster zu identifizieren und zu verstehen. Kapitel 5 zeigt auf wie HLC Daten dabei helfen können, die geschichtliche Entwicklung einer Landschaft zu erforschen.

Kapitel 6 gibt einen Ausblick auf die mögliche Entwicklung der ländlichen Regionen in Devon. Mit Hilfe von HLC werden verschiedene Entwicklungen des 20sten Jahrhunderts wiedergegeben, unter besonderer Berücksichtigung gefährdeter Landschaftstypen. Es wird aufgezeigt, wie die Ergebnisse des HLC Projektes dazu beitragen können, ländliche Gegenden zu erhalten und zu verbessern.

Claudia Dürrwächter

Key to HLC maps in this book

	Historic settlement		
	Modern settlement		
Strip fields		Public complex	
Medieval strip-enclosures		Industrial complex	
Medieval enclosures (from strip fields)		Mining	
Medieval enclosures		Quarries	
Barton fields		Military complex	
Post-med enclosures (strips)		Former military complex	
Post-medieval enclosures		Airfield	
Post-medieval enclosures with medieval elements		Former airfield	
Post-medieval enclosures from rough ground		Dunes	
Horticulture		Sand or pebbles	
Orchard		Rock	
Former orchards		Mud	
Park/garden		Mud & sand	
Watermeadow		Marsh	
Post-medieval watermeadow		Water	
Ancient woodland		Modern enclosures	
Other woodland		Modern enclosures replacing industrial	
Conifers		Modern enclosures replacing parkland	
Woodland with old field boundaries		Modern enclosures replacing postmed watermeadow	
Rough ground		Modern enclosures replacing medieval watermeadow	
Rough ground with earlier fields		Modern enclosures replacing woodland	
Rough ground with mining remains		Modern enclosures from rough ground	
Rough ground with prehistoric remains		Modern enclosures adapting post-medieval fields	
Recreation		Modern enclosures adapting medieval fields	

CHAPTER 1

REGIONALITY AND THE CHARACTER
OF BRITAIN'S LANDSCAPE

This short book has two purposes. Firstly, I have written it to present the results of the Devon Historic Landscape Characterisation (HLC) project, undertaken between 2001–5 with sponsorship from English Heritage and Devon County Council. You can find the HLC on the internet *via* http://www.devon.gov.uk (see Chapter 2 for more details; or you can consult the archive version at the offices of the Devon County Council Historic Environment Service, who are currently located at County Hall in Exeter).

Secondly, I hope it will serve as an introduction to Devon's wonderfully rich and endlessly fascinating historic landscape (fig. 1). As such, it has two introductory chapters. In this chapter, I will discuss the historic character of Britain's principal landscape regions, and outline how the historic landscape of Devon compares with other parts of the country. In Chapter 2, I give an introduction to the development of Historic Landscape Characterisation, and describe the methodology we adopted for the Devon HLC project.

WHAT IS THE HISTORIC LANDSCAPE?

As I write this I am sitting on a train, speeding down the East Coast Mainline from Newcastle towards York – and then on to the South West. As I look east out of the window, the English landscape unfolds before me in the early morning light. The train has just crossed the border into Yorkshire from County Durham; in the distance, the North York Moors are barely visible through the grey gloom of a January day. The fields, hedges, farms and villages that flash past me are all part of the 'historic landscape'. They are all here as a direct result of people's lives and work over thousands of years. Some features are quite recent, like the streetlights still twinkling in the small town we have just passed through; others are more ancient, like the earthworks of ridge and furrow that roll even now across some of the fields here in the Vale of York. The combination of local minutiae creates a distinctive stretch of country that is not quite like any other. All the physical features and local details in this landscape are historic – together they make up today's human habitat: an historic, cultural landscape shaped over millennia by the people of the past and present (fig. 2).

Our understanding of historic landscapes and what they mean to us has developed a great deal over the last fifty years. In the 1950s, the celebrated archaeologist O.G.S. Crawford made a powerful analogy between the landscape and a 'palimpsest' – a piece of vellum overwritten many times with different texts. His words are often quoted by archaeologists, since he was among the first to outline the potential of ordinary landscapes for our discipline. According to Crawford, the landscape is like:

> ... a document that has been written on and erased over and over again; and it is
> the business of the field archaeologist to decipher it. The features concerned are

Fig. 1.   Middlecott Farm, Chagford, Dartmoor, 1982.
© Chris Chapman, by kind permission.

of course the field boundaries, the woods, the farms and other habitations, and all the other products of human labour; these are the letters and words inscribed on the land. But it is not always easy to read them because, whereas the vellum document was seldom wiped clean more than once or twice, the land has been subject to continual change throughout the ages.

(Crawford 1953: 51)

At the time he was writing, this comparison between the landscape and a historical document would have been immediately understandable to Crawford's academic contemporaries: most of them had trained as historians rather than archaeologists. However, it was from about this time onwards that scholars of the English landscape like W.G. Hoskins, H.P.R. Finberg, M.W. Beresford and J.G. Hurst increasingly pursued the physical remains of the past in their research.

As a result of their pioneering work, the importance of the 'historic landscape' was well established for archaeologists by the 1980s and 90s. Their studies had also begun to influence wider agendas. There was an increasing awareness in government and amongst the public that something valuable was lost when features like hedges or old farm buildings were destroyed. Research like Stephen Rippon's Gwent Levels Project was able to show that historic landscape archaeology could be used to inform and influence large-scale planning

Fig. 2. South Northumberland's coastal plain from the air. The particular combination of elements in this historic landscape – like medieval ridge and furrow, large post-medieval fields, extensive opencast and deep coal mines, settlements of the industrial period, long sandy beaches – create a distinctive and individual landscape. Photo: Sam Turner, November 2005.

of major infrastructure projects, in this particular case the route of a new motorway. In his report, Rippon outlined what he regarded as the historic landscape:

> . . . the last cultural layer, that is the present pattern of fields, roads, and settlement.
>
> (Rippon 1996: 1)

His intention was perhaps to differentiate 'historic landscape' from *buried* archaeology, and in doing so to ensure that the visible, standing and still-used vestiges of the past received separate and thorough consideration in the planning process. This definition was followed in some of the earliest Historic Landscape Characterisation projects sponsored by English Heritage. Today, informed by the developing perspectives of landscape archaeology and cultural geography, we can widen our definition of the 'historic landscape' to include more. We know that the way we value places depends not only on what we can see, but also on *how* we see them. A place that has witnessed particular events in the past will always be regarded differently by people who know about those events – battlefields are an excellent example. We can broaden our frame of reference to include all those elements that contribute to landscape character, encompassing not only the features we still use, but also earthworks or field remains of long-deserted sites. By means of a range of archaeological

3

Fig. 3.   Berber Hill, Kenn. The photograph shows how the distant past influences the present, and how different types of evidence can help us understand the landscape. Cropmarks of boundary ditches belonging to a prehistoric hill-top enclosure are visible as slightly darker green lines in the grass. The later field boundaries – which are probably medieval – have (partly) followed the line of these defences. Photo: Frances Griffith/DCC, 29/6/1984.

techniques we can integrate barely visible or even wholly buried features into our analyses, like the soilmarks or cropmarks left by ancient settlements (fig. 3), or earlier landscapes concealed beneath recent alluvial deposits. When we know they are present, both physical remains and cultural associations can change the way we see the land: they become part of the historic landscape.

THE CHARACTER OF BRITAIN'S RURAL LANDSCAPES

My train will arrive shortly at Birmingham. I have passed through many different types of historic landscape: the great, regular fields of the eastern counties bordered by thin, spindly hedges; the Derbyshire hills dusted with snow, their drystone walls snaking darkly up to the horizon; quarries and abandoned industrial sites now overgrown with scrubby woodland. But in the last fifty miles or so I have not only seen a range of different land-uses: I have also passed across the boundary between two of Britain's most important landscape zones: from the 'planned' to the 'ancient' countryside.

The broad distinctions between different English landscapes have been recognised for centuries. Long before archaeology became a subject in its own right, the English topographers of the 16th century appreciated the distinction between the 'countries' of 'champion', at that time dominated by large open fields, and those of 'woodland', where then as now thick hedges and little patches of woodland divided up the farming landscape into small compartments (Williamson 2003). The same distinction was recognised by

Maitland in the 19th century, who used extracts from two 1st edition Ordnance Survey maps to highlight the contrasts (one from the Devon-Somerset border, the other where southern Oxfordshire bordered Berkshire across the Thames; Maitland 1897; Rackham 1986: 1). Subsequent writers like W.G. Hoskins (1963) and Oliver Rackham have developed these perspectives further. In his classic book *The History of the Countryside* (1986), Rackham mapped what he saw as the dividing lines between the three principal landscape zones of England (fig. 4). In the South East he defined a triangle of 'ancient countryside' extending from the Hampshire coast in a north-easterly direction along the line of the Chilterns into Suffolk and Norfolk. Another belt of 'ancient countryside' covered west Dorset, east Devon, and Somerset, together with the counties of the West Midlands and the North West. In between these two zones, a broad band of 'planned countryside' stretched from central Dorset all the way up to North and East Yorkshire. Finally, he labelled the uplands of the Pennines, the Lake District, the North York Moors, the Welsh marches and the South West (including almost all of Devon) as the 'Highland Zone'.

Rackham identified certain features that he regarded as typical of the 'planned' and 'ancient' countrysides. In the former, the settlement pattern was characterised by nucleated

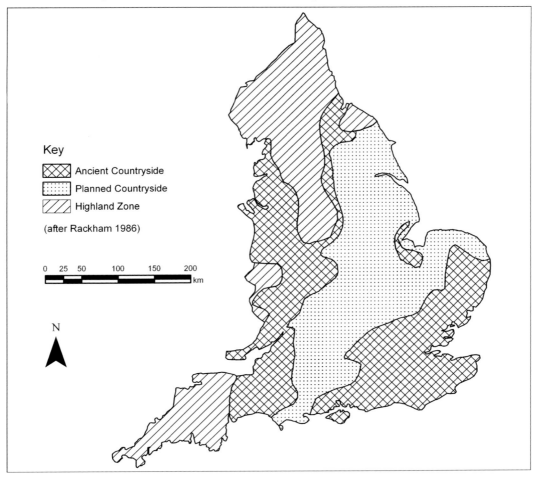

Key

[×××] Ancient Countryside

[:::::] Planned Countryside

[////] Highland Zone

(after Rackham 1986)

0   25   50   100   150   200
km

N

Fig. 4.   The three main landscape zones of England, as defined by Oliver Rackham (1986).
(Redrawn by Sarah Lynch).

villages and occasional isolated farms. The fields were often rectilinear, their flimsy boundaries dominated by a handful of species like hawthorn and blackthorn. The roads between them tended to be wide and straight, and on the surface - at the same level as the fields (1986: 4).

By contrast, the landscape of the 'ancient countryside' was much less regular. People lived dispersed in small hamlets and frequent isolated farms, amid a chaotic patchwork of little fields with thick, sinuous hedges composed of many species. There were plenty of small patches of woodland, and the roads and tracks that linked all these features together cut down into deep hollows after centuries of continuous use (1986: 4).

Meanwhile the 'Highland Zone' was a mixture of these characteristics and others. Principally, of course, there were large areas of unenclosed and unfarmed moorland (just how much becomes obvious if, instead of taking the train, you fly from Exeter to Newcastle on a clear day). There were also large areas of parliamentary enclosure in many upland regions, especially in the north of England.

When discussing the fundamental divisions between 'ancient' and 'planned' countryside, Rackham also highlighted the date the characteristic features of each landscape type first emerged (Rackham 1986: 4-5). The most important differences were probably between the settlement patterns and field systems of the two zones. In the 'planned countryside', many field systems were re-planned as regular, straight-sided enclosures during the 18th and 19th centuries. Prior to this, the landscape had been dominated by large open fields, though it was not uncommon for a process of piecemeal enclosure to have eaten away at this medieval pattern in the early modern period (Williamson 2000). The vestiges of earlier field patterns are often still present in the form of ridge and furrow earthworks, whose patterns can be used to model the arrangement of the medieval landscape (Foard *et al.* 2005). The tracks between settlements were commonly regularised at the same time, creating the broad, straight roads familiar today. The settlements here classically fall into two categories: villages, perhaps established between AD *c.*850-1200, and isolated farms created in the 18th and 19th centuries. The result of all this post-medieval re-planning is that much of today's 'planned countryside' is only a few hundred years old, though it often perpetuates elements from earlier times.

Rackham's 'ancient countryside' presents rather a different picture. Here the landscape had often been fully enclosed by the 16th century: so long ago that few traces of how it happened remain in the surviving documentary records. It is becoming increasingly clear that many of the fields had once been divided into open strips in this region too, but they disappeared much earlier than in the 'planned countryside' (Herring 2006a). Although we do not really know when most medieval settlements in Devon were first established, documents, excavation and archaeological survey show that it was certainly during the Middle Ages; analogy with Cornwall suggests it could have been as early as the 7th to 9th centuries. Most of the roads and tracks in these areas seem to have existed by the time the fields were enclosed. 'Ancient' really is an appropriate word to describe such a landscape.

We can identify some problems with Rackham's generalisation. One is that it tends to over-simplify the story of each region's landscapes. He wrote, for example, that:

> ... slight research will show the [ancient countryside] is the product of at least a thousand years of continuity and most of it has altered little since 1700 ...
>
> (Rackham 1986: 5)

Whilst this is true in some respects – particularly if we compare the 'ancient' to the 'planned countryside' – we should not take it too literally. No landscape that has been inhabited for a thousand years is just the same as it was a thousand years ago, even in the most conservative of societies (Turner 2004). In Devon, subtle variations in the environment and the cultural and economic lives of the people have created the differences that now distinguish the character of one area from that of its neighbours. Since 1700, these changes have included the enclosure of heaths and downland, the modification of existing fields, the establishment of conifer plantations, and the growth of extractive industries like mining and quarrying (see Chapter 4).

When he put Devon in the Highland Zone, Rackham was drawing on a scholarly tradition that led back through Hoskins (1963) and Sir Cyril Fox (1938) to Maitland and beyond. Maps like Rackham's present deliberately broad generalisations, and we should not criticise them too much for problems with particular details. They have been extremely useful to landscape historians because they have helped them to identify important questions and problems for future research.

Indeed, the division between the 'ancient' and 'planned' countrysides seems in general terms to be a valid one. It is supported by scholars who have recognised similar distinctions from a range of different sources. In the 1960s, Joan Thirsk used the testimony of written documents like wills to create maps of early modern farming regions. Her work clearly showed that the agriculture of the South West peninsula differed from its eastern neighbours in the 16th and 17th centuries (1967). This strongly suggests that different agricultural practices might lie behind some of the contrasts we see in today's historic landscape.

More recently, Brian Roberts and Stuart Wrathmell have pioneered a method based on analysing historic settlement patterns depicted on 19th century Ordnance Survey maps (2000; 2002). Like Rackham they identified three principal regions in the English landscape, though their lines were drawn in slightly different places. Roberts and Wrathmell's 'Central Province' largely corresponds to Rackham's 'planned countryside', though it reaches up beyond the Tees to include County Durham and Northumberland. Their 'South-Eastern Province' is similar to Rackham's south-eastern 'ancient countryside', but their 'Northern and Western Province' also includes much of his 'Highland Zone'. By identifying a number of sub-regions in each 'Province' they were able to separate contrasting areas like the Devon moors and lowlands. Overall, this makes for a more satisfactory characterisation because it is richer in detail. However, because their focus was settlement patterns, they did not say much about the form of fields and other types of land-use in each of their sub-regions. I hope the research undertaken for this book will show that HLC can take the process on another step by identifying the combinations of historic landscape types that give each area of the rural landscape its particular character (see Chapter 5).

DEVON'S PLACE IN BRITAIN'S LANDSCAPE

Most historians and archaeologists agree that the character of Devon's historic landscape is rather different to that of most other parts of England. But to date, there has been relatively little concurrence on how we might understand, categorise and look after these everyday rural landscapes. We are now beginning to see the complex relationships between different land-use types, though the histories of their development are still not thoroughly understood.

Travelling through Devon along Brunel's Great Western Railway serves to emphasise a problem with including most of the county in the 'Highland Zone'. The train from Taunton to Plymouth snakes along fertile valleys scattered with settlements and tangled with ancient fields and hedgebanks. A journey like this shows how dissimilar most of Devon is to the barren uplands of the Pennines or the North York Moors. There are high moors in the county, of course: Exmoor and Dartmoor preserve some of the 'wildest' territory in the south of England. But elsewhere, in the South Hams and between the moors, there are many miles of fertile farmland. This has much more in common with the 'ancient countryside' Rackham identified to the east – and historically, there was just as much rough grazing ground in east Devon as in other parts of the county. Most of lowland Devon is dominated by ancient enclosures, so in this book I have treated it as a kind of 'ancient countryside'. Chapter 3 discusses the character of Devon's fields and their historical development.

A persistent problem, obvious from many previous studies, is that the divisions between the different English landscape regions are not absolute. Piecemeal enclosures in the 'planned countryside' disrupt the regular post-medieval pattern; old winding roads and occasional hamlets betray a more complicated medieval picture. In south Devon, Thirsk's map showed a band of 'sheep-corn' country along the south coast: here we find nucleated villages and large, regular fields more akin to those of the midlands than their neighbours 10 miles inland (Thirsk 1967). In north Devon, the regular post-medieval enclosures cut from the heaths and moors are more like the parliamentary enclosures of the 'planned countryside' than the sinuous, curving boundaries of the medieval farmland they border. One of the fundamental characteristics of the Devon landscape is that a mixture of many

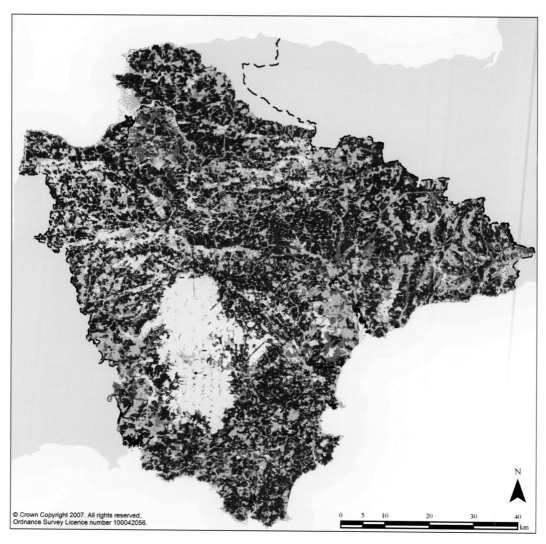

0   5   10   20   30   40
km

N

Fig. 5.   The Historic Landscape Characterisation of Devon, *c.*1890:
a complex mix of various landscape types.

landscape types is often found interdigitated in complex patterns (Williamson 2002: 118) (fig. 5). In Chapter 4, I discuss the histories of some of the most important historic land-use types, including orchards, watermeadows, woodland and rough ground. Using the HLC can help us to map these variations and interrelationships in more detail than most other large-scale techniques. In Chapter 5, I try to show how it can help us to appreciate the patterns in the past that lie behind them.

Finally, in Chapter 6 I will consider the future of Devon's historic rural landscape. I will use the HLC data to look at some trajectories of change in the 20th century, in particular by focusing on vulnerable landscape types. I hope to show that the HLC project could make a useful contribution to the conservation and enhancement of the rural landscape, and to debates on the preservation and reinforcement of local distinctiveness in the future.

CHAPTER 2

UNDERSTANDING HISTORIC LANDSCAPES:
ARCHAEOLOGY AND HISTORIC LANDSCAPE CHARACTER

LANDSCAPE ARCHAEOLOGY AND HISTORIC LANDSCAPE CHARACTER

There is a long tradition of research into the landscape archaeology and landscape history of England. The first part of this chapter explains how the approach I have taken in this book fits with archaeology in general and how it developed, before going on to look in more detail at the methods I have used to map the historic character of Devon's landscape.

Archaeology is the study of the human past through its material remains. This includes not only the things people made, but also the remains of their bodies and those of other living things they grew, ate, or lived amongst. The idea of 'landscape' is an important one for archaeologists. Clive Gamble makes this clear in his recent introduction to archaeology:

> Archaeology is basically about three things: objects, landscapes and what we make of them. (Gamble 2001: 15).

At the most basic level, landscape archaeologists collect information about sites and land-use in the past, and study the relationships between them. Beyond this, though, different archaeologists have different ideas about the *significance* of landscapes and how we should interpret them, not only as far as the people of the past are concerned, but also for people in the present.

Various trends in historical and archaeological thought had a significant impact on the development of landscape archaeology in Britain (Johnson 2005). First, there were pioneers like O.G.S. Crawford, H.P.R. Finberg and W.G. Hoskins, who from the 1920s onwards realised that the archaeology of the English landscape presented a complicated web of elements from different historical periods that could be unpicked with care to reveal its historical development (Hoskins 1955). These men all had interests in south-west England, and Finberg and Hoskins in particular worked extensively on Devon (Finberg 1951; Hoskins 1954) (fig. 6). As the 20th century wore on, research in this tradition was criticised for not incorporating new developments in archaeological theory. However we regard their work now, though, men like Hoskins and Finberg laid many crucial scholarly foundations, particularly for the study of historic landscapes.

From the 1950s onwards the so-called 'new' archaeologists promoted the study of landscapes as economic resources. In 'new' archaeology, scientific techniques and statistical methods were applied to retrieving and analysing archaeological remains in order to understand economic systems better. This movement came under sustained attack in the 1980s and 90s from other archaeologists who emphasised the importance of social and cultural aspects of past landscapes. Some of these focussed on understanding how the

Fig. 6. H.P.R.Finberg's map of Tavistock. Finberg's map presents a characterisation of the landscape in the medieval parish of Tavistock based on 18th-century map sources and earlier documents. It shows Tavistock at the centre of an area of cultivated land, with extensive tracts of moorland and woodland lying at its margins. (From: H. Finberg, 1951. *Tavistock Abbey*, (Cambridge), facing page 41. Reproduced by kind permission of Cambridge University Press).

organisation of the landscape reflects past societies, whilst others have stressed the way that landscapes are cultural constructions expressing particular cultural meanings.

Increasingly, we have realised that many different approaches can give us useful insights into past societies. Today's archaeologists appreciate that we need to examine entire landscapes from a range of perspectives when we are trying to answer the big questions about the past, and not just concentrate on individual elements like sacred sites or food production techniques (e.g. Dommelen 1999: 284; Given *et al.* 1999). This means we have to get our data from different sources and combine them to create rich descriptions of past societies. One of the most important achievements of recent social and cultural approaches to archaeology is the realisation that the whole landscape both affects and is affected by people (Knapp & Ashmore 1999: 20-1; Crumley 1999: 270). One of the implications is that if we want to approach past societies through the landscape we need to have as much information available as possible: not just data about the location of individual archaeological sites, but also about what lies in between them. We have to put sites into a richer context than we can by simply plotting a few points on a map, and we need to try to encompass whole landscapes.

Secondly, the theoretical battles between different intellectual and political movements in the 20th century have taught us that there is more than one way to see the same landscape. Agreement is not always easily won. We cannot expect our interpretations of the landscape to be final or definitive: someone will always see things a different way from us, either because they have new information, or just because they are coming from a different perspective. Landscapes, like so much else, are in some ways a matter of perception. What we 'see' in a particular landscape depends to a great extent on our social, economic and cultural background, our academic or professional training, and our personal interests (Olwig 2004). Even relatively similar people can see the same place in many different ways. Contrast, for example, the perspectives of three different people looking at the same field (fig. 7). As an archaeologist, I tend to notice any earthworks that are present, and look carefully at the form of the boundary: things that tell me something about the history of the field. My cousin is a zoologist, and she looks at the field in terms of habitat – what species

Fig. 7.   View towards Iddesleigh and Dartmoor, Iddesleigh, Devon *c.*1985.
Photograph by James Ravilious (copyright James Ravilious).

might the grassland or hedges support, and what level of biodiversity. My mother, on the other hand, is a farmer: when she looks at the same field, she will see the different grasses growing and can tell how good the field will be for grazing her livestock. She also happens to love wild flowers, so she will particularly notice these when she checks the hedges and fences to see how easily her sheep or cattle might escape.

We all give the landscape different meanings when we look at it, and these meanings inevitably depend on our perceptions and perspectives. Despite this, our perceptions of the landscape are not entirely arbitrary, but instead they are rooted in the material things that we all see, work with and live amongst (Olwig 2004; Widgren 2004). Because archaeology involves the study of material things, we can use an 'archaeological' approach to bring together different people's perspectives on the same landscape (Turner 2006b).

If we are trying to accommodate many different views, we must accept that there will be debate and argument between people about what aspects of the landscape we value most. The importance and relative merits of different landscapes have been contested throughout history, and we continue to argue over them today (Hall 2006). Particular interest groups clash over the best way to use, conserve or change landscapes depending on their aims. Archaeologists' responses to these new problems must be quick and flexible. To meet these new challenges, we need a new way of presenting and analysing the whole historic landscape (Turner & Fairclough, forthcoming).

The way we understand and value landscapes affects how we change them. This is just as true for people today as for people in the past. Landscape archaeology should have something to contribute not only to understanding how people lived in past landscapes, but also to managing landscapes today and planning them for the future (see Chapter 6; and Turner & Fairclough, forthcoming).

THE DEVELOPMENT OF HISTORIC LANDSCAPE CHARACTERISATION

In England in the early 1990s there was a growing realisation that despite some success in the conservation and management of individual historic sites and monuments, the broader historic landscape was being ignored (Fairclough *et al.* 2002: 69-70). English Heritage therefore commissioned a research project to evaluate and compare different methods for understanding and valuing the historic landscape. These included techniques where experts delimited areas of landscape based on the distribution of monuments they considered to have particular historical and archaeological significance, and methods that tried to assign some kind of value to the whole historic landscape (Fairclough *et al.* 1999; for examples of differing approaches see respectively Darvill *et al.* 1993 and Herring 1998: 7-8). As a result of this work, English Heritage sponsored further research by Cornwall Archaeological Unit and its partners who undertook the first large-scale Historic Landscape Characterisation (HLC) work on Bodmin Moor in late 1993, subsequently extended to cover the whole county in 1994 (Countryside Commission 1994; CCC 1994; CCC 1996).

HLC is a method for mapping, presenting and understanding the landscape with reference to its historical development (McNab & Lambrick 1999: 54). HLC maps differ from traditional methods for describing the historic landscape in several important ways, though like them HLCs are used for both landscape management and research. By 'traditional methods' I mean archaeological databases of sites and monuments like county-based Historic Environment Records (HERs) or English Heritage's National Monuments Record (NMR). Generally speaking, HERs and the NMR provide lists of archaeological sites together with relevant information about each one, including their physical location (fig. 8). Some of these databases are now very sophisticated and contain a great deal of archaeological information; many UK HERs are available in whole or in part to interested members of the public over the internet (e.g. Somerset (SCC, n.d.); Tyne and Wear (Sitelines, n.d.)). As inventories of sites they are crucial tools for research, planning

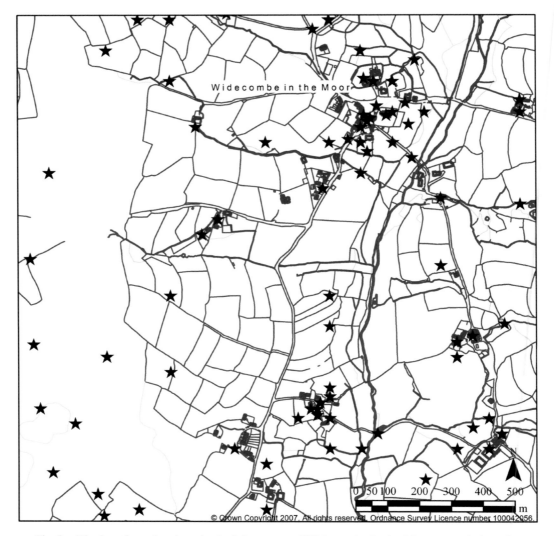

Fig. 8.   The location of archaeological sites around Widecombe in the Moor recorded on the
Devon Historic Environment Record and plotted as 'point data' (black stars) against
the modern digital Ordnance Survey Land-Line® map.

and landscape management, particularly where the preservation and enhancement of
individual sites and monuments is concerned. However, there are some significant problems
with these databases. Firstly, the information they contain about site location is usually
limited to a dot or a line on a map. Even when the full extent of a feature or site is shown
there is normally little information about the surrounding landscape. This means it is hard
to appreciate the individual monument as part of a historic landscape, either in the present
or the past. Secondly, whilst HERs continue to record sites in ever greater numbers, they
can never record *everything* of historic interest in any given locality. If archaeologists and
the public were only interested in great monuments like barrows, hillforts, Roman camps,
and medieval castles the HER officer's job would be relatively easy. As it is, people have
come to realise that it is not only these major monuments that give places their special

14

Fig. 9.   Sites from recent periods, like this derelict farm building at Lidwell in the Tamar valley, are being included more and more on Historic Environment Records. Photo: Sam Turner, July 2006.

qualities, and so HERs have expanded to include more and more different types of sites: features with relatively recent origins such as cottages, milestones, chapels, mining remains, farmsteads, lanes and gateposts all now feature regularly in archaeological inventories (fig. 9). Today, we know that the unique character of individual places does not necessarily come from associations with a famous or important site, but might just as well arise from the special combination of features in a place: the houses, gardens, hedges, lanes, trees, woods and fields that make up the landscapes we see. To record all these features in an HER would be impossible: it would take many years of detailed research to make records of all the buildings, hedges, trees and lanes in a single Devon parish, let alone the whole county.

Historic Landscape Characterisation provides one way to help deal with these problems. Unlike an archaeological inventory, HLC does *not* map individual archaeological features. Instead, it groups together features like field boundaries, lanes and farms that are linked by their historical development and then maps them as areas. To do this, the HLC researcher needs to understand how patterns in the landscape reflect its historical development, and how the physical features that make up the landscape relate to one another (Fig. 10). So like all landscape archaeology, HLC mapping involves a process of interpretation that is informed by the physical landscape.

HLC uses mapping techniques that generalise the features in a given area based on certain characteristics. Similar techniques have been used in other disciplines for years – for example in geology to show soil types, or in ecology to map habitats. HLC is perhaps most closely related to 'Landscape Character Assessment (LCA)', a technique developed by landscape architects in the 1980s and 90s. The two can be used together, and HLCs are often designed to add an extra level of detail for planners using LCAs to make decisions about future landscapes. However, the two systems are not the same. For a start, HLC tends to work on a smaller scale than LCA, and it maps defined historic landscape character types that recur, rather than individually unique character areas (Fairclough & Macinnes 2003). HLC has little concern for pure aesthetics, but instead it brings the historicity of the landscape to the fore. It emphasises how modern (and earlier) landscape character is the result of history's 'long chain' of events (Fairclough 2003).

HLC recognises that all parts of the landscape have historical significance which is the result of human activity and use over the millennia. Peter Herring, who played an important role in developing the HLC methodology in Cornwall, described the basis of the method developed there as follows:

> Closer examination [of the landscape] reveals that particular groupings and patterns of components which recur throughout the county can be seen to have been determined by similar histories. Cornwall's historic landscape can, therefore, be characterised, mapped and described, using a finite number of categories or types of "historic landscape character".

(Herring 1998: 11)

Fig. 10.   An historic landscape: an aerial view of the landscape of the Blackdown Hills, looking west across Luppitt Common. The sinuous boundaries of medieval enclosures lie on the valley sides and valley bottom; straight-sided post-medieval fields have been laid out on Luppitt Common above (part of the Common still lay unenclosed at the beginning of the 20th century). The settlements of Greenway Farm (centre left, with smoke rising) and Luppitt (extreme right) were both first mentioned in Domesday Book, where they were recorded as small estates of one and two hides respectively in 1066 (Thorn & Thorn 1985: 23,19 and 23,20).
Photo: Sam Turner, November 2005.

In practice this means that the present-day landscape is examined using modern Ordnance Survey maps and characterised according to the features present into landscape 'types'. These 'types' are classified in advance of mapping and are defined by the broad characteristics exhibited by areas of land with similar past uses. In the Cornwall HLC, Peter Herring and his colleagues defined seventeen landscape 'types' in fairly broad categories, for example rough ground, medieval enclosures, post-medieval enclosures, ancient woodland, ornamental, and industrial (Herring 1999: 21).

HLC 'types' are then mapped using GIS (Fairclough 2002). In different areas of the country, different 'types' will be appropriate because of differing landscape histories, or because the landscape characterisation has been designed to be used at a larger or smaller scale. The HLC method can therefore be very flexible. In Cornwall, characterisations of localised study areas have been undertaken at 1:10,000 and 1:2,500 scale using HLC 'types' designed for individual projects (Herring 1998: 20-1; Turner 2006a) (fig. 11).

As with all archaeological work, HLC raises certain methodological problems. One of these is the difficulty of consistently identifying areas in the 'correct' categories. Even when a project is undertaken by a single researcher, it is possible for areas with similar historic characteristics to end up mapped as different 'types'. This may just be the result of error, but sometimes it is difficult to decide which 'type' a given block of landscape belongs in. One way to manage this problem is to base the pre-defined character types on a wide range of well researched case-studies (like the examples presented for some of the character types discussed in Chapter 3). A related problem is that some areas may include features from several different eras that contribute strongly to overall character, so that it is unclear which

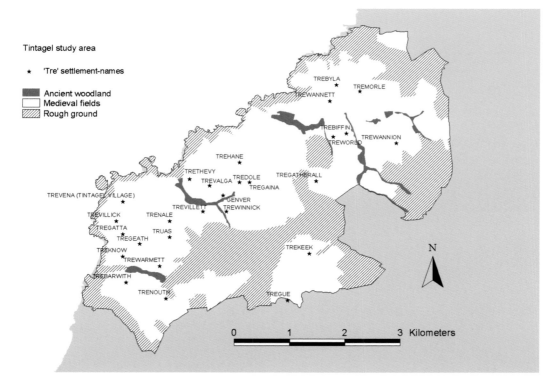

Fig. 11. An HLC of part of Cornwall, intended to represent aspects of medieval land use and settlement in the area around Tintagel (see Turner 2006a: 71-106).

'type' should be mapped. This consideration also leads to problems associated with 'time-depth': a 'recent' landscape (for example, one created by enclosure in the 19th century) may conceal strong elements of another kind of landscape (e.g. prehistoric or medieval enclosures). Various techniques have been tried to overcome this difficulty, but using GIS along with some explanatory text probably allows the most flexible solution (Herring 1999: 22). GIS systems are much more adaptable than conventional paper maps, because they allow the user to include and map many pieces of information in relation to each individual feature or area. In modern HLCs like the Devon project, using a database linked to a GIS allows a range of attributes to be held for each individual block of each character type. This means the user can build up a relatively detailed picture of the historical development of the landscape. It can also enable us to map how fast and to what degree the landscape character of a given area has changed over time.

In the conclusion to their recent book *Hedgerow History: Ecology, History and Landscape Character*, Gerry Barnes and Tom Williamson have made some useful criticisms of the HLC method (Barnes and Williamson 2006: 137-140). They argue that one of the problems with HLC is its reliance on air photographs and maps, which means it does not get down to ground level to experience the landscape from the position of a real person. In this sense, they go on, HLC is out of kilter with recent archaeological approaches that try to approach past sites and landscapes from the perspectives of the people of the past – on the ground (see e.g. Barrett 1994). By producing characterisations based on maps, so Barnes and Williamson argue, we miss the real local value given to the landscape by the different plants that grow in hedges and other boundaries, and by a failure to appreciate local styles of wall building or fencing (fig. 12). As an example, they point to the hawthorn hedges of north-west Norfolk and the Scots pine 'rows' of Breckland: both have their origins in the

Fig. 12. A local walling style: stone-faced boundaries in Peter Tavy parish, on the western edge of Dartmoor. Photo: Sam Turner, July 2006.

later post-medieval period, and both were normally planted on straight boundaries, yet the different plants give quite a different character to their respective regions. They argue that an HLC would not pick up this difference, so 'characterisation' is something of a misnomer for HLC, since 'character' is based on more than just the date of enclosure.

These are perfectly valid criticisms of many large-scale HLC projects. It can be difficult to address issues like varying hedgerow composition properly through a county HLC. The scale and sources used in the recent large-scale projects sponsored by English Heritage and Historic Scotland means it can be hard to include data about the field boundaries themselves, or about every different type of habitat encountered. Even historic Ordnance Survey maps generally include little information about boundary composition, and on modern printed OS maps it is normally impossible to differentiate hedges from walls, or banks from wire fences (unlike their French equivalents, the new maps in the 1:25,000 *Série Bleue* of the Institut Géographique National: these do at least show whether a boundary is a hedge, a wall or a fence). Vertical air photography is slightly more useful – we can at least normally tell a barbed wire fence from a hedge (fig. 13). Even so, it is often impossible to work out certain details: whether a hedgebank is faced with stone, for example, or the height of a wall and the way it was built.

This is largely to do with the scale at which individual projects have been undertaken rather than the methodology itself. In some ways, we might like to undertake the kind of detailed field survey that Barnes and Williamson have done in Norfolk before producing

Fig. 13. Vertical air photograph showing different boundary types: Devon hedgebanks and wire fences around the deserted farmstead at Kerraton, Rattery.
Photo: © getmapping, 2000 (compare figs 15, 16 and 137).

an HLC for any area. Such ambitious work is normally impossible because of the time constraints on HLC projects, which often have to cover whole counties or regions in one or two years' work. It would be hugely expensive and time-consuming to do detailed, field-based surveys for all types of boundaries in all parts of a county, or even for a sample like the Norfolk one. Instead, HLC projects like Devon's rely on a limited number of case-studies and field visits to provide analogies that can be used to help interpret the wider landscape.

This does not mean, however, that HLCs cannot be adapted to include perspectives other than those presented here. One of HLC's strengths is its ability to include a wide range of perspectives on the same area. Because the data is held in a GIS, it is easy to add data or change the information linked to each unit. We could even add new interpretations or new data to HLCs that have already been 'completed'. HLC is not a monolithic approach, and different workers might choose to characterise the same area in different ways; there is no reason they should not (Williamson 2006: 57-9). HLC-type approaches do not seek to present 'official' histories of landscapes. Instead, they are open to claims and counter-claims, providing a forum for debate and negotiation about the significance of the historic landscape (Turner 2006b).

No one methodology or source can summarise every aspect of a place, and neither HLC nor other archaeological or historical techniques claim to do so. If we want a real in-depth understanding of a particular place, we need to bring together a wide range of sources and different types of data. These problems are increasingly being recognised by the people whose job it is to manage and conserve the countryside. For example, the UK's Highways Agency has recently produced a set of guidelines on the historic landscape to be taken into account when new roads are being planned and built (Highways Agency 2006). The guidelines clearly describe how specialists from different disciplines – archaeologists, buildings historians, landscape architects, landscape historians and so on – need to work with one another to bring together their different perspectives on a particular area. In this way, all the elements that give an area its special character can be considered when a road is being planned so that the negative impacts can be minimised and opportunities for enhancement can be grasped. If we want to use HLC to help understand, manage and plan landscapes, it is important that we integrate its perspectives with information from other sources and with the views of other people.

THE DEVON HLC METHOD

Since the first Cornwall HLC was finished in 1994, English Heritage has encouraged HLC projects across much of the rest of England (Fairclough & Wigley 2005). In the South West, HLCs for Somerset and Exmoor National Park were finished in 2001 (Aldred 2001), and at the time of writing one for Dorset is almost complete.

Mapping for the Devon HLC was concluded in January 2005. It was undertaken by the present writer, who was working then for Devon County Council's Historic Environment Service. The following paragraphs present a brief account of the methodology used, but a more detailed description can be found in the project report (Turner 2005). Devon is a large county, and the HLC covers well over 6,000km^2. This includes Dartmoor National Park and the unitary authorities of Plymouth and Torbay, though it excludes the part of Devon in Exmoor National Park which was mapped during the Somerset HLC project.

The GIS chosen for the project was ESRI's ArcView 3.2. When we began in 2001 this was the industry standard desktop package. The data relating to each individual block of a specific landscape character 'type' (known as a 'polygon', or a 'geometry') were initially recorded and then stored using a Microsoft Access database (fig. 14).

The project has used three principal sources to inform the characterisation, all of which were incorporated into the project GIS at the outset:

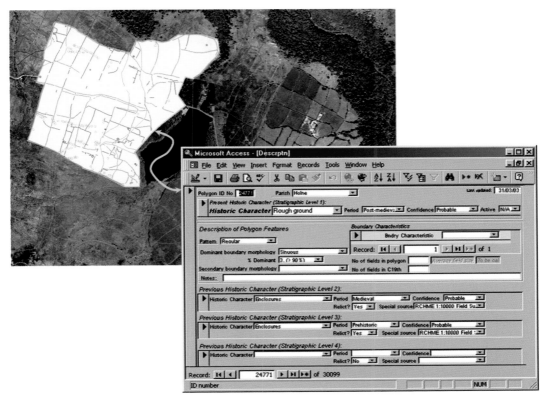

Fig. 14. A screenshot showing an HLC polygon on Holne Moor and its associated entry in the project database. The coloured lines within the polygon represent the results of English Heritage's 1:10,000 scale field survey of archaeological earthworks on this moorland, with prehistoric (red), medieval (green) and post-medieval (blue) features. Photo: © getmapping, 2000.

1. Ordnance Survey Land-Line® (modern map, available as an electronic vector dataset for use in GIS; fig. 15).
2. Ordnance Survey 1st edition 6 inch (1:10,560) or 25 inch (1:2,500) maps (in Devon, these date mostly to the late 1880s and early 1890s. They are now available as an electronic raster dataset from Landmark Information Group Ltd (fig. 16). In a few places there are gaps in the digital 1st edition coverage where original maps have been lost or destroyed; in these cases the 2nd edition, dating to the first decade of the 20th century, was used instead).
3. Vertical colour air photography, supplied by getmapping.com. These photos were taken between 1999-2000, and were available as an electronic raster dataset (fig. 13).

Using GIS each of these datasets can be superimposed on any of the others, so it is quick and easy to compare them. Certain other datasets were also available, and were incorporated where appropriate. For example, the English Heritage Survey Division (formerly the Royal Commission on the Historical Monuments of England) has undertaken field survey at 1:10,000 using GPS of archaeological remains surviving on much of the upland region of Dartmoor. This data was used together with the vertical air photography to provide an extra level of information about areas with extensive visible earthwork remains on the Moor.

The HLC mapping was undertaken at a scale of around 1:10,000, and should be used at

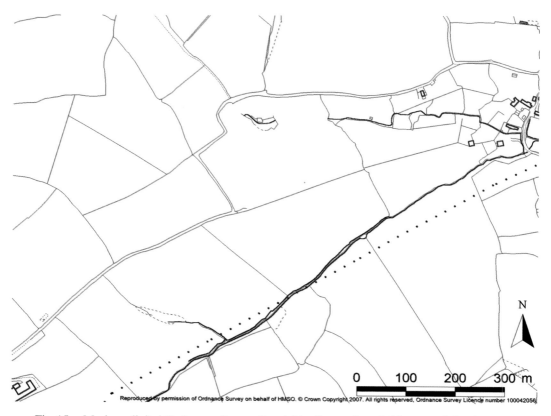

Fig. 15.   Modern digital Ordnance Survey Land-Line® map data: fields around the deserted
farmstead at Kerraton, Rattery (compare figs 13 and 16).

1:25,000 or smaller. The smallest individual 'polygons' mapped were theoretically 1 hectare
in area (100m x 100m), so the project can provide a detailed model of Devon's historic
landscape character. The finished database contains around 50,000 individual polygons.

The whole area included in each 'polygon' had to be composed of the same historic
character type in today's landscape. As far as could be ascertained from the available
sources, it must also have shared the same historic character type (or the same sequence of
different types) throughout its history. Of course, we sometimes find very small patches of
particular land-use types. For example, in areas like the Tamar Valley tiny scraps of mining
remains – the tops of shafts, ruined buildings and so on – often exist in fields and woodland.
Where they fall below the 1 hectare threshold, these are not included in the characterisation,
which is after all intended to be a broad-brush exercise. However, many will be included in
other databases as individual monuments (e.g. the county HER), so their contribution to
landscape character will not be entirely lost to holistic studies of the landscape. Normally,
the HLC works at a bigger scale than this, and the overall average size for polygons is about
13 hectares.

As far as possible, the number of different HLC types was kept to a minimum in the
Devon HLC in order to make the database more user-friendly. At the most basic level, the
data can be displayed in the GIS to show where very simple categories of land-use lie: fields,
woods, rough ground, parks and so on. However, in order to reflect the subtle variations
in the county's historic landscape other information has also been added to the database.

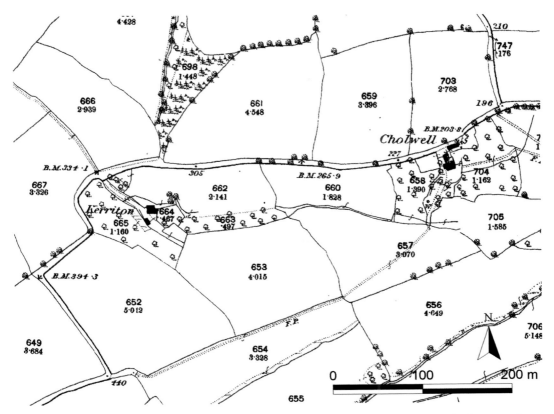

Fig. 16. First edition 1:2,500 Ordnance Survey map data (*c.*1890): fields around a farmstead at Kerraton, Rattery (compare figs 13 and 15). Map reproduced by kind permission of Landmark. © and database right Crown copyright and Landmark Information Group Ltd (all rights reserved 2007).

Because we can combine different variables to create maps using GIS, we can draw on all the data recorded in the database to create more complex maps for a range of purposes.

For example, the form of fields created at different times are subtly different to one another (as explained in Chapter 3). Most of Devon's landscape today is covered with fields, but categorising them by period of origin based on their boundary morphology alone can be fraught with problems. Some HLC projects have tried to develop 'objective' methods that interpret the landscape according to quantifiable criteria. In Somerset, for example, field types were categorised according to the straightness or curviness of the field boundaries in a given block of land (Aldred 2001). This distinction is important because we know that most field boundaries first created after about 1750 were surveyed and straight (Williamson 2002; Barnes & Williamson 2006: 60-2). The Devon HLC database also records this kind of information, including the relative proportion of straight to sinuous boundaries in each polygon, and the regularity of the pattern they form (Turner 2005; fig. 17).

Used on its own this kind of strictly 'morphological' approach risks ignoring important but rather subtle variations between different landscape types, for example the many types of enclosure that share sinuous field boundaries. These can be very hard to distinguish: it is not even clear that developments reflected in field and boundary morphology followed uniform paths in different parts of Devon. Any 'reading' of historical processes based

23

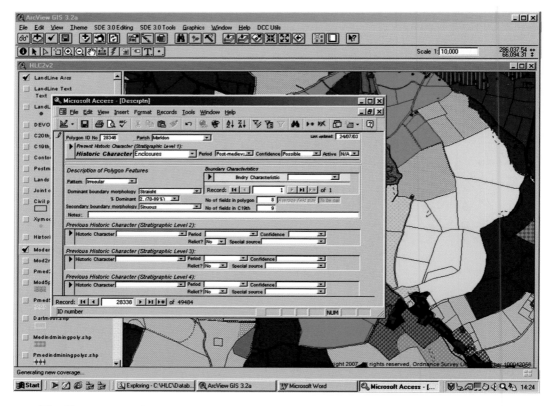

Fig. 17. A screenshot of the GIS and database in preparation. The record for the polygon highlighted bright yellow is displayed in the database window. The image illustrates how morphological information about each polygon was recorded (e.g. the relative proportion of straight to sinuous boundaries, and regularity/irregularity of the pattern of boundaries).

solely on morphology will normally give us identifications that are approximate at best, particularly for a large-scale study like the Devon HLC.

In an attempt to counteract some of these problems, the Devon HLC has also used case studies of landscapes drawn from published archaeological and historical research. These enabled the identification of a range of historic landscape character types in advance of mapping. HLC types were then assigned based largely on analogies with the case-studies.

In the HLC database, both 'objective' and more 'subjective' data are recorded for each polygon. Using GIS we can create maps to display this information in many combinations. An added benefit of this approach is that the Devon HLC data can be mapped against neighbouring counties using their own terms. One of HLC's strengths is that the method is easy to adapt to suit local conditions, but this sometimes means it is difficult to make comparisons at a regional scale (Williamson 2006: 59). The data recorded in the Devon project was designed to make it possible to compare the county with both Cornwall to the west and Somerset to the east.

One of the principles of HLC is that it recognises the dynamic quality of landscapes. Landscapes have always changed, and they will continue to do so through human action and natural processes. However, not all landscapes change at the same speed or in the same ways. Whether we are engaged in research, day-to-day management or planning for the future, it can be useful to see how landscapes have changed in the past.

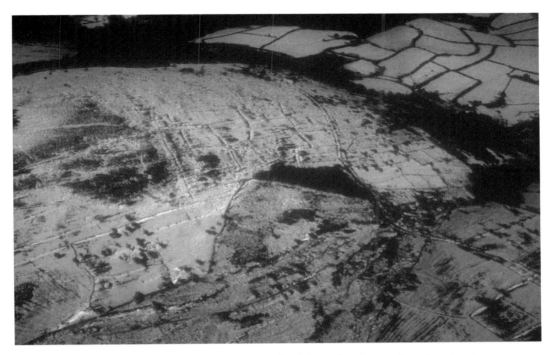

Fig.18.   An air photograph of part of Holne Moor, showing earthworks of various periods, including Bronze Age field boundaries and medieval ridge and furrow (bottom right). Photo: Frances Griffith/DCC (Holne Moor SX67 17th March 1985).

In order to reflect changes in historic character through time, the Devon HLC database was designed to allow a sequence of character types to be recorded for each 'polygon' (fig. 14). First, the present-day character type was recorded based on the evidence from air photos and the modern Ordnance Survey maps. Second, an interpretation of the late 19th-century landscape character was made based on the 1st edition OS maps. In addition, when I could make a confident interpretation of earlier historic character types this was also added to the database. These interpretations were based on the historic characteristics of each area in the 19th and 20th centuries. In practical terms, this meant relevant archaeological features had to be visible within the polygon. These normally take one of two forms. Firstly, there might be earthworks, ruins or other remains that indicated former character and use. So, for example, the vestiges of medieval ridge-and-furrow lying within what was rough moorland in the 19th and 20th centuries would be recorded in the database entry for that polygon (fig. 18). Secondly, the way the landscape was organised in earlier times can often be discerned from the arrangement of boundaries and other features in more recent landscapes. In this way we can be fairly sure that areas of medieval strip field farming once covered much of the farmland now occupied with great, curving hedgebanks (as discussed at greater length in Chapter 3. See also Herring 2006a). Using this feature of the database, the HLC user can map modern, post-medieval and earlier land-use and landscape character on a county-wide scale. This means we can not only model earlier patterns of land-use, but we can also trace which landscapes have remained most stable and which have changed fastest.

DEVON HLC: INTERNET VERSION

To make the HLC accessible to people in Devon and beyond, Devon County Council Historic Environment Service published the results of the project on the internet in 2007 at this address:

http://www.devon.gov.uk/index/environment/historic_environment/landscapes/landscape-characterisation.htm

It is accessible to anyone using a standard internet browser through a web-GIS. Users can view the data at different scales with a range of appropriate Ordnance Survey maps as background. They can view both original, unprocessed data as collected during the project, and also processed versions after some basic analyses – for example, to represent the character of Devon's landscape as it was *c.* 1890. We hope this will be useful and interesting to both residents and visitors. Readers of this book, for example, could use the web GIS to view the HLC for the places discussed in the text.

CHAPTER 3

DEVON'S FIELDS: ORIGINS, DEVELOPMENT
AND HISTORIC CHARACTER

INTRODUCTION

Devon is a farming county now just as it has been for thousands of years, and most of its landscape is covered with fields. The special character of the countryside here is intimately linked to farming. Picture, for example, a great hedgebank in May, draped in primroses, bluebells, and campions, snaking alongside a little sunken lane between the spring pastures: nothing evokes the unique spirit of Devon's landscape more intensely. These fields and hedges are not here because nature has made them, but because farmers have been working the land for hundreds and thousands of years – the efforts of countless past generations still give the countryside its character today. Careful research by landscape historians and archaeologists has shown that we can distinguish fields created at certain times by their shapes and sizes. This chapter introduces the principal types of fields mapped as part of the Devon HLC, and looks at a selection of well-known examples to illustrate when they originated and how they developed. The amount of space I have dedicated to each character type roughly reflects the area of Devon it takes up.

A broad-brush study like the Devon HLC cannot normally tell the exact year or even century when a certain farm's fields were created. This can be hard to work out using any methodology, let alone one designed to provide a general overview of a whole county. Nor can it tell us when fields came into or went out of use for a specific agricultural purpose: for this we need much more detailed studies of historical sources like medieval and post-medieval texts or archaeological evidence like ancient pollen. The strength of the HLC is that it helps us understand today's landscape and its development on a wider scale, and shows the broad periods when field systems originated or changed significantly. It shows how today's countryside is made up of a complex mosaic of pieces whose origins lie in many periods.

Change is one of the principal characteristics of any landscape whether it is rapid or incremental. Even when people do not make major alterations, natural processes lead to slower changes: trees and plants still grow and die, ditches silt up, streams and rivers change their courses. For these reasons, it is perhaps a little misleading to talk about 'medieval' landscapes in Devon today: no landscape is still just as it was 500 years ago. Even if it was, people's ideas and perceptions have changed totally since then, so we still would not see things the same way our ancestors did.

On the other hand, some areas retain stronger influences from their past than others. Archaeologists suspect that some areas of roughly parallel historic field banks are likely to incorporate elements of prehistoric field systems. We know about these from Dartmoor, where boundaries known as 'reaves' dating to the Bronze Age once enclosed great areas of fields (see Chapter 4). In other parts of England, landscape historians have identified extensive areas of field systems that may perpetuate the general layout of the later prehistoric countryside (Williamson 1998), and there is no particular reason why elements of similar systems should not also have survived in Devon. Indeed, archaeological excavations in the east Devon lowlands have revealed the fragmentary remains of field systems now lost on the surface, some of which had regular parallel boundaries rather like the Bronze Age reaves (Fitzpatrick *et al.* 1999). In the rolling landscape north and west of Crediton, roughly parallel hedgebanks run across the fertile countryside for considerable distances. We know from Anglo-Saxon land charters that some of these were used as the boundaries of small estates in the early Middle Ages, like the one running between Ruxford Barton and West Sandford; the tenth- and eleventh-century farmers might well have been re-using earlier lines in the landscape (Hooke 1994). Very occasionally, the remains of prehistoric field systems survive as earthworks in land that was later used for pasture, as on the thin limestone soils between Torbay and Dartmoor (Gallant *et al.* 1985). None of these have been excavated, so the exact date they were first created is uncertain. Whilst the later first millennium BC is often suggested, settlement and farming in Devon during the Roman period continued much as before; sites like the Roman-British settlement enclosure at Stoke Gabriel are also surrounded by small irregular fields (Griffith 1988: 57).

Because the Devon HLC has tried to map earlier landscape character where this was possible, we can often detect the long term trends in the way the county's landscape has changed over the centuries. This does not usually extend back into prehistory, but it does often allow us to detect where landscape character has remained relatively stable and where it has changed fastest, particularly from the Middle Ages onwards.

THE FORM OF DEVON'S FIELD BOUNDARIES

Some of the most stable features in rural Devon are its fields. To be sure, these have seen many modifications and changes, with different crops, farming practices and changing land uses all subtly altering their appearance and value. Despite these modifications, the boundaries of many fields still follow the same lines they did 500 or even 1000 years ago. A brief look at the form of south-western field boundaries serves to illustrate how much today's fields owe to their predecessors, as well as some of the ways they differ from them.

In a county the size of Devon, we can find many different types of boundaries around fields, woods, parks and farms. Fences are relatively uncommon, and yet there must be many thouands of kilometres of different sorts: barbed-wire fences dividing up modern fields where old boundaries have been destroyed; wooden fences keeping horses in their new suburban paddocks; even long 19th-century metal railing fences in a few places, as at Castle Hill Park (Filleigh). Walls are more common, especially on the uplands of Dartmoor, where the drystone wall dividing up the highland pasture is a familiar feature of the moorland scene. Despite their often ramshackle appearance and the way they seem to fit so naturally into their surroundings, simple drystone boundaries in Devon are almost all relatively recent structures: most belong to the 'improvements' of the 18th and 19th centuries. Much more common throughout Devon are banks with stone-built facings, which themselves are a subset of the most widespread boundary-type in the South West, the 'Devon' hedge (known in Cornwall, of course, as the 'Cornish' hedge). These great earthen banks, normally planted on top with woody species to form a raised hedge, are the commonest built feature of the rural landscape in both counties.

It seems that the tradition of building such hedgebanks has its roots way back in prehistory, at the time the earliest major land divisions were created by people in Devon. The earliest Bronze Age 'reaves' of Dartmoor included stretches of bank and ditch, as at Shaugh Moor and Holne Moor (Smith *et al.* 1981; Fleming 1994a). In their earliest phases these boundaries were sometimes simple post-built fences, but stone or stone and earth banks later became the norm. In places, prehistoric boundaries underlie medieval and modern hedgebanks. There are many likely examples around the southern and eastern fringes of Dartmoor (discussed in Chapters 4 and 5), and prehistoric field systems elsewhere have also influenced the pattern of later landscapes. There is a good example at Deckler's Cliff (East Portlemouth) on the south coast of Devon, where a prehistoric field system now preserved in rough cliff-top grazing lies on much the same alignment as the medieval and later field boundaries running away to the north (Newman 2003). Away from Dartmoor, archaeologists have identified relatively few upstanding prehistoric boundaries in Devon. A small number are known on Exmoor, where most surviving areas of prehistoric fields come from the high central moorland (Riley & Wilson-North 2001: 40-44). Archaeologists working between the rivers Dart and Teign in south Devon have found earthworks of early field systems that survive up to about half a metre high: they have tentatively assigned them to the prehistoric period, but this is not certain (Gallant *et al.* 1985).

We have learnt from excavations of Romano-British examples in Cornwall that a field boundary might begin as a wall and later turn into a substantial bank when stones cleared from the fields and soil from ditches were thrown up against it (Herring 1993). So even where field boundaries like these have very old roots, the way they look today results from both recent management practices and how they have developed over the course of their long history. Many field boundaries first created in prehistory or the Middle Ages will look quite different now compared to how they did 2000 or even 500 years ago. It also seems that medieval farmers had a range of options at their disposal when they were enclosing their fields, so we should not expect all Devon's old field boundaries to look the same. In fact, archaeological work has shown that it is extremely hard to distinguish field boundaries of different dates in the South West based on their modern structure alone, except for some types first built in the last 200 years or so. The archaeological evidence from pipeline and road construction projects in Cornwall suggests that many hedgebanks originated as fairly small medieval features that were later enlarged. Linear development projects like pipelines often slice through large numbers of historic field boundaries, allowing archaeologists to record and compare many such features as part of a single project. The work of the Cornwall Archaeological Unit has shown that it is often possible to trace a complicated sequence of development with several phases, and many large hedgebanks only reached their present size in the 18th or 19th centuries (fig. 19). Such boundaries quite often seal deposits of ancient soil, which can be analysed by specialists for information about the landscape and local environment before enclosure. Unfortunately, relatively few Devon hedgebanks have been recorded in this way. Whilst some projects linked to new developments are beginning to include hedgebank recording, it is vital that future work always records the form of boundaries (including detailed records of sections through hedges when they are opened) and the plant species present in the hedge.

Much archaeological work recording Devon's early field boundaries has been done on the moors, and to an extent the results recorded there reflect the range of lowland boundary types too (Fleming and Ralph 1982; Newman 1994). The majority are variations on the simple earthen hedgebank, though in areas where surface stone is very plentiful, banks of stone are sometimes present (fig. 12). The banks themselves vary in height, width and construction methods depending on a range of factors – research in Cornwall has shown that these probably include the age of a boundary, but certainly also relate to the local geology, farming practice and so on (Bull 1998; Herring 2006b). They are sometimes faced on one or both sides with stone, and the specific style of this facing appears to depend very much on local preference and available materials. Whilst some stone-faced banks are clearly medieval, others were originally simple earthen structures that did not get their facing walls until the post-medieval period. Ditches are common in some areas, but not in others – though of course if not regularly cleared out they may have silted up since they were first constructed.

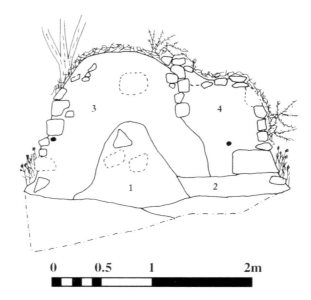

0   0.5   1   2m

Fig. 19.   Section of a hedgebank at Godolphin, Cornwall showing four phases of development (CHES 2001, fig. 23. Reproduced by kind permission of Cornwall Historic Environment Service).

Most of Devon's hedgebanks are topped by great growing hedges. Typically they contain a varied mix of species and as such provide a marvellous haven for wildlife (fig. 20). It was once thought that, subject to certain caveats, the number of woody species present in a 30-metre length of hedge could provide a rough guide to its age, with perhaps one new species colonising the hedge every hundred years or so. However, detailed work by researchers including Stephen Cousins in Northumberland and Gerry Barnes and Tom Williamson in Norfolk has shown that this is not the case (Cousins 2004; Barnes & Williamson 2006; see also Muir & Muir 1987: 48-75). In some places, hedges planted in the last two hundred years or so are likely to contain fewer species than older hedges. However, there are many other factors besides age that have to be taken into account. The most important is probably the local soil conditions, which appear to have a major impact on species diversity in both recent and ancient hedges in counties like Norfolk. In addition, boundaries were often planted originally with more than one species, and hedges that lie on roadsides or mark the outer limits of a field system (as opposed to internal sub-divisions) also tend to be species-rich.

Hedgerow surveys in various parts of Devon have shown that age is not necessarily related to the number or variety of species present. In fact, many Devon hedges are rich in woody species whatever their age, probably because they were planted with more than one species from the start. Around the end of the 18th century, agricultural writers like Vancouver were recording the planting of mixed hedges in the South West, and many post-medieval boundaries will contain a significant diversity of species (Vancouver 1808). Documentary research and hedge survey undertaken by archaeologists before the construction of Roadford Reservoir north-west of Dartmoor revealed that hedges planted in both the 19th century and the 1930s contained on average about same number of species as all other hedges – around six per thirty-pace stretch of hedge (Boldon 1988). The survey results showed that the botanical mixture of hedges had most to do with soil conditions and topographical location, with plants like oak, sallow, birch, rowan, guilder rose and alder buckthorn commonly occurring together in wetter areas; ash, sycamore and beech were common on drier soils. The importance of soil conditions has been highlighted by other

Fig. 20. A recently-laid hedgebank on Colston Farm, near Buckfastleigh. Standard trees have been left at intervals; the wire fence is protecting the restored hedge until it becomes stockproof. Photo: Sam Turner, July 2006.

research in Devon, for example at Farley Farm near Chudleigh, south-east of Dartmoor (Michelmore & Proctor 1994). All the hedges surveyed here are probably ancient – they all pre-date the earliest surviving 19th-century maps of the farm. The combinations of species that made up each hedge appeared to reflect to a large extent the siting of the boundary and the soil where it was constructed. This chimes well with work from the east of England that has highlighted the importance of soil and climate (Barnes and Williamson 2006). It is not clear that detailed survey of hedgerow species in Devon will help us work out when the surviving fieldscape was first created, or indeed how it has been altered over the course of its long history. However, detailed recording of sample hedgerows in the county's many different regions would provide a valuable resource for managing future change in the countryside, and for mapping the relationships between farming and the natural environment. It will inform the perspectives gained from HLC by adding another dimension to our understanding of landscape character. If this work can be linked to palaeoenvironmental research into the nature of ancient vegetation, we may start to get a better understanding of how much plant communities in our hedges have changed over the last thousand years or so.

Field boundaries are the commonest features used to interpret the historic character of agricultural land in the Devon HLC. Because the project was dealing with areas rather than individual monuments, no individual boundary defined an area as belonging to a specific character type. Instead, the HLC maps combinations of boundaries that together give an area its historic character. An area mapped in the HLC as 'enclosures with medieval origins' may well include later or earlier features, whether boundaries or different classes of monuments. It is important to remember that other features may well have existed in the area in the past, and that the configuration of hedgebanks, buildings, walls (or whatever) may well have been modified significantly over the years. Nevertheless, the historic character of an area mapped as 'enclosures with medieval origins' in the HLC will be derived principally from its use as enclosed fields during the Middle Ages.

FIELDS WITH MEDIEVAL ORIGINS

It seems likely that most of the farmed land in medieval Devon and Cornwall was divided into strip fields (Herring 2006a). As their name suggests, these were large fields subdivided into long, narrow strips of land. On average, strips were probably about 30m wide and between 140-200m long. They were commonly separated by low earth or stone baulks (Herring 2006a, figs 26 & 33; 2006b, fig. 38). In turn the strips could be subdivided by ridges and furrows, though evidence for these does not often survive in Devon (Herring 2006b). Each strip could have been farmed by different people, so that neighbours' land lay intermixed in the fields. Most strip fields underwent major changes in the later Middle Ages, when they were normally enclosed with banks, ditches and hedges. This often left distinctive 'markers' behind in field boundaries and field patterns, such as bundles of narrow strip enclosures, or so-called 'reversed-s' or 'reversed-j' curves (discussed below). Strip fields of different sorts were enclosed in Devon from the 13th century (and probably earlier) until the 19th century. Archaeological and historical studies suggest that the straightness or curviness of field boundaries and the shapes of the fields can throw some light onto the processes and dates they were created. Nevertheless, it is worth stressing that the original date field patterns were laid out is only provisionally intepreted in the Devon HLC; in virtually all cases it could be improved or confirmed by more detailed research.

For the purposes of the Devon HLC and this book, I have divided field-types with medieval origins into five main categories:

1. Strip fields
2. Strip enclosures
3. Enclosures (based on strip fields)
4. Other medieval enclosures
5. Watermeadow

The first four of these are described in this chapter, with examples to show how and when they developed. Watermeadows are discussed further in Chapter 4.

Strip Fields

Today, surviving strip fields form only a tiny percentage of Devon's historic landscape. Despite this, they are worth discussing in some detail because their influence on Devon's landscape character has been immense. Indeed, it is no exaggeration to say that it would be virtually impossible to understand the historic landscape of Devon and many other western regions without considering them first. It seems that they were once virtually ubiquitous; they are the shadowy predecessors of much of the medieval and modern countryside.

In most people's imaginations, the classic medieval countryside probably features a village with a manor house and church surrounded by great open fields. This familiar image is based on studies from the 'champion' lands – the English Midlands discussed in Chapter 1, or continental regions like the plains of the Paris Basin or Burgundy in France (e.g. Chouquer 1993). The characteristics of such a landscape are large villages and open fields divided up into arable strips, extending out beyond the edges of the settlement as far as the eye can see. Although virtually all have been enclosed in England, there are still extensive areas of open strip fields elsewhere in Europe and beyond. In many places the strips have been amalgamated into large unenclosed fields under single ownership, but there are still

Fig. 21.   An landscape with large, open subdivided fields in Galicia, north-west Spain.
Photo: Sarah Semple, May 2005.

Fig. 22.   Devon's enclosed landscape in drought: looking south-west across Denbury
hillfort (with woodland, centre left) towards the Dart valley and the South Hams.
Photo: Frances Griffith/DCC, SX86 Denbury, 18th July 1989.

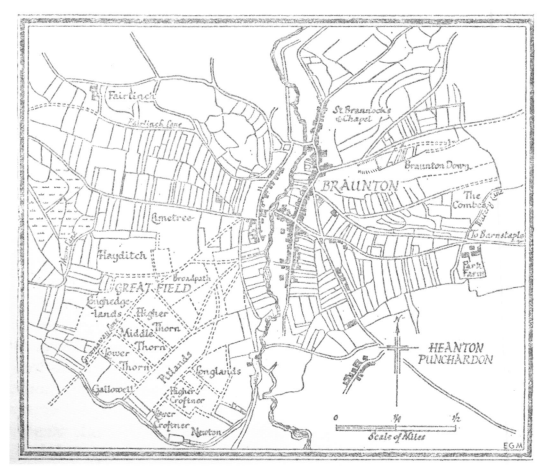

Fig. 23.   H.P.R. Finberg's plan of Braunton Great Field
(Finberg 1949; reproduced by kind permission of *Antiquity* Publications Ltd).

many regions where the land around villages or hamlets is still divided into strip fields today (fig. 21). The countryside of Devon seems totally different to these open landscapes. There are farms and hamlets scattered everywhere, and the dense tangle of lanes and hedgebanks that hem in the fields seems quite at odds with the landscape of the champion regions (fig. 22). Even so, the work of archaeologists and historical geographers continues to reveal two important facts: firstly, that much of the structure of today's rural landscape in Devon and Cornwall does indeed have its origins in the medieval period; secondly that it was once much more open than today, and that almost everywhere the farmland was formerly divided into strip fields.

Landscape historians have recognised that Devon was once a county of strip fields since the mid-20th century, though the idea has been curiously slow to gain general acceptance. It was H.P.R. Finberg, one of Devon's greatest historians, who drew attention to evidence preserved in early documents and maps that clearly showed how fields in many localities were once split into strips. His seminal article in the archaeology journal *Antiquity* highlighted the case of Braunton in north Devon (Finberg 1949; 1969) (figs 23 & 24). The

Fig. 24. An aerial view of Braunton Great Field. Photo: Frances Griffith DCC 18th December 1985.

north bank of the Taw estuary is hardly the place we might expect to find one of the finest surviving examples of a medieval open field in Britain, yet here is Braunton Great Field, lying to the south-west of the village between the River Caen and the dunes of Braunton Burrows. The field is still divided into strips, whose boundaries have historically been marked by low turf banks known as *landsherds* (though far fewer survive today than were recorded at the beginning of the 20th century). Using a document of 1324, Finberg was able to show that the arable strips in the field were held as intermixed parcels during the Middle Ages, proving Braunton was a true open field. Other evidence, considered below, shows that the remains of related systems survive in a few places elsewhere in Devon.

It remains unclear whether it was common for 'open' field systems like Braunton to be *completely* open – i.e. unenclosed by perimeter hedgebanks or fences. Comparison with other parts of south-west England suggests that the medieval open fields were probably surrounded by long, irregular outer boundaries. These are mentioned in documentary sources from the late Anglo-Saxon period onwards in areas that we know were dominated by open field agriculture. Features such as hedges, banks and ditches are mentioned in several descriptions of estate boundaries dating to before the Norman Conquest. These documents were often attached to land grants and described a route around the periphery of an estate. In Somerset, Dorset and Cornwall the boundary descriptions in numerous charters contain references to a *dic* (this normally signifies a ditch and bank; Costen 1994: 104). The example of Trerice in Cornwall may be particularly relevant here (Herring &

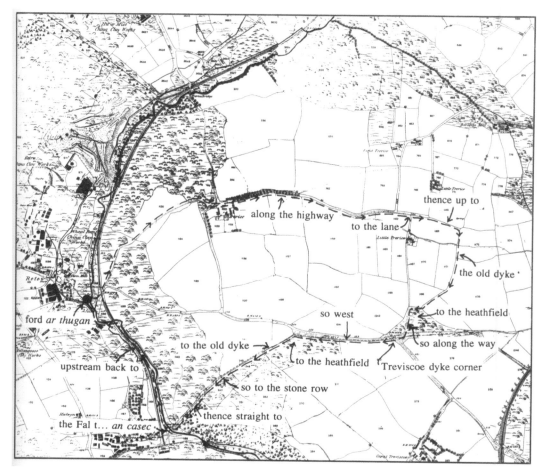

Fig. 25. The charter boundary clause and historic landscape of Trerice (Cornwall), as interpreted by Peter Herring and Della Hooke (Herring & Hooke 1993: 69).

Hooke 1993) (fig. 25). As in much of Devon, this part of central Cornwall has historically been dominated by a pattern of scattered farms and small hamlets which almost certainly has its origins in the period AD 500-1000 (Turner 2006a, 71-98). The charter boundary-clause of Trerice, compiled when the estate was granted by King Edward (the Confessor) to his 'faithful minister' Eadulf in AD 1049, contains references to 'old dykes' in two places (Sawyer 1968, no.1019). At the end of the charter is an addition stating that 'the enclosures (*worþigas*), the barley land and the out-leap are common (*gemæne*).' The 'enclosures' referred to here are probably the little closes immediately around the farmsteads, and the 'out-leap' seems likely to have been unenclosed rough grazing ground (Herring & Hooke 1993: 74). By studying the later medieval fields that lay within the charter boundary we can see they are enclosures based on strips within the formerly common 'barley land'. In Devon, 'dykes', 'old dykes' and 'boundary hedges' occur in charters at various places, and they might well have marked the outer boundary of common field systems too (for example at Littleham, Dawlish and Ottery St Mary; Hooke 1994: 200-212).

A later medieval example showing how strip-fields could be enclosed by irregular,

36

Fig. 26. Part of the RCHME field survey of Challacombe (Manaton) overlaid on a vertical air photograph (© getmapping, 2000). The yellow lines represent lynchets and other boundaries in the historic field system.

sinuous boundaries comes from Challacombe on the eastern side of Dartmoor. Through a lucky combination of surviving archaeological remains and post-medieval map evidence, we can form a good impression of how a small strip field system on the high moors must have looked (Pattison 1999). Certain land holdings at Challacombe were still a detached part of the manor of Kenton when a detailed survey was made in the late 18th century. Even though Kenton is some 27km to the east on the Exe estuary, this is a relationship whose origins probably lie in the Anglo-Saxon period, when the moorland would have provided summer grazing for livestock (Fox 2005). A map of Challacombe that was attached to the survey shows that the strips in the fields were still held between several different owners in 1787. In a few fields holdings had been consolidated under a single owner, but in the majority of the *wares* (fields) around the settlement the *landscores* (the local name for the strips) of individual proprietors lay intermingled with their neighbours' land.

Archaeological evidence of lynchets and banks derived from field survey and aerial photography shows not only that the strips depicted on the map have survived as earthworks, but also that many others once existed both within and outside the boundaries shown on the 1787 map. A recent survey by the Royal Commission on the Historical Monuments of England (RCHME, now part of English Heritage) revealed much new detail about the field system, and showed what a complex multi-period landscape the archaeology preserves at Challacombe (fig. 26). For example, at the north-west corner of the RCHME's survey area,

Fig. 27.   Modern Ordnance Survey Land-Line® map of Challacombe.

long narrow fields of probable medieval date lay over part of a prehistoric settlement, and these were in turn cut by other, later strip field ploughing. Just over Challacombe Down from here, the late- or post-medieval tin mining openwork of Scudley Beam seems to cut into the fields north of the medieval settlement (Newman 2006, fig. 59). The settlement of Challacombe itself, now just a single farm and a row of cottages, was once a hamlet of perhaps seven tenements.

It is particularly important to note that the large subdivided fields, or *wares*, are bounded by irregular, sinuous boundaries. Though historians once thought these must have been later than the open strip fields, the RCHME's survey showed that this was probably not the case (Bonney 1971; Pattison 1999: 68). Across the little West Webburn River at East Challacombe, the former strip fields are also enclosed within long, curving outer banks, though here these large enclosures are sub-divided by more recent field walls. On Bodmin Moor in Cornwall, Peter Herring has identified similar outer enclosures around the earliest fields of the settlement at Brown Willy (Herring 2006b).

The evidence from Challacombe shows several things. Firstly, the outer enclosures of blocks of strips could well be medieval in date and might have been established when the fields were first laid out; they need not have been enclosed only in more recent centuries. Secondly, the archaeology shows that blocks of strips grouped together could form subrectangular fields with only slightly curving boundaries. If all that survived at Challacombe was the outer boundaries of the large fields, without the 1787 map and the

Fig. 28.   A vertical air photograph of Godsworthy, on the western edge of Dartmoor. In strong oblique sunlight, the earthworks of former strip divisions are visible in the fields, running up and down the slope. The boundaries of other fields, now abandoned, can just be made out in the surrounding rough ground. Photo: © getmapping, 2000.

surviving earthworks, it seems highly unlikely that we would have recognised it as a strip field system (fig. 27). Finally, the fields here show beyond doubt that there were small common field systems in operation in medieval and later Devon. Individual proprietors' lands were intermixed in strips in a similar way to those of bigger open fields like Braunton, just on a much smaller scale and presumably with rather simpler rules.

Oddly, the fields at Challacombe are not typical of south-western strip fields in one important way. Many (though not all) of the lynchets here run *along* the contour. This was the normal arrangement in many other parts of Wessex to the east, and medieval lynchets on plenty of hillsides in Somerset, Dorset and elsewhere bear witness to this. By contrast, in Devon and Cornwall the normal orientation for strips was *up and down* the slope (Herring 2006a). This is clear from the gentle curves of strips preserved as later boundaries in many places (these are discussed later in this section), and also from earthwork examples like Godsworthy (Peter Tavy), where strong oblique sunlight reveals the slight earthworks of former strip boundaries (fig. 28).

So certain types of archaeological and written evidence show that both large open fields like those of Midland England and smaller common strip fields existed in Devon during the Middle Ages. However, not all strip fields were also *common* fields, and some – perhaps many – seem to have been made up of large blocks of contiguous strips that all belonged to one owner. This seems particularly likely on demesne land, that is to say the fields of a manor that belonged directly to the manorial lord (Alcock 1975). But even high on the moors, where there were relatively few tenants, land was farmed in a similar way (Brandon 1979; Austin *et al.* 1980). The fields were still ploughed in ridges and furrows, which naturally led to the formation of strips. These might not have been held communally, but the look of the land would have been much the same. Though rare in Devon compared to the counties of the Central Province, such ridge and furrow does still survive in a few places, particularly on the uplands of Dartmoor. This may be because post-medieval agriculture has been less intensive here than in the lowlands, so the ridge and furrow is less likely to have been destroyed by later farmers (fig. 18).

Outfield strips

We normally think of open strip fields as the core agricultural land belonging to a settlement or manor, and in Midland regions like Northamptonshire this was usually the case (for a mapped region see Foard *et al.* 2005). However, in Devon archaeological evidence or historical records of strips do not always refer to regularly cultivated 'inland' arable in core areas. Research by the landscape historian Harold Fox has shown that periodically cultivated land known as 'outfield' could also be divided into strips in medieval and post-medieval Devon (Fox 1973). The main uses for outfield were as rough pasture for beasts, and for products like furze and heather, which were used in Devon and Cornwall for fuel, fodder and litter (Herring 2004: 45-7). However, the outfields were also periodically ploughed, after which they were sowed with crops and used to supplement the arable production of the ordinary 'inland' fields. There may have been particularly intensive cultivation of the outfields in Devon during the 13th to early 14th centuries, the 16th century and the mid-18th to 19th centuries (Fox 1973). Whilst these periods may have seen the most frequent

Fig. 29.   Traces of post-medieval ridge and furrow agriculture are visible in many places on Dartmoor, as here just above Dunnabridge (earthworks running across the foreground of the photograph). Photo: Sam Turner, June 2004.

Fig. 30.   Combe, Lifton. Slight lynchets of strip divisions are visible on Tinhay Down (centre left).
Photo: Sam Turner, May 2003.

activity, outfield was also used intermittently at other times for crops, though the intervals between episodes of ploughing could be amazingly long, in some places between 30 and 50 years.

Documents from Kenton manor dating to the 16th century and later show that there were two main types of outfield (Fox 1973). The simplest was held in 'severalty', which means that individual blocks of land belonged to individual farms, like Ash Heathfield and Kenwood on the lower eastern slopes of Haldon. More complex and more interesting were 'common' outfields. In Kenton these included the commons of Warborough, Cofford, Great Western and Hayton. None of these remain as open land today, since all have either been enclosed or planted with conifers. On a map of 1783, however, the commons appeared as islands of open field strips in between the farms' enclosures. This is because in effect they were a form of irregular open field – just one that was cultivated very infrequently. 16th-century documents tell us that the strips were divided by 'ancient boundmarks' or 'landmarkes', probably low banks of earth or stones like the *landsherds* in Braunton Great Field. When the outfield was cultivated, each tenant returned to their strips in the field, which lay intermixed with those of their neighbours. At other times – sometimes for whole lifetimes – no crops were planted and beasts were allowed to wander and graze across the common (Fox 1973).

Outfields like this, either held in common or privately, were once widespread in Devon. It used to be thought that they were either a sort of hang-over from some primitive 'Celtic' agricultural practice, or a half-way point on an assumed road to a fully 'developed' system like that of the Midlands, or else were the result of unfavourable conditions for farming in the South West. Harold Fox has shown that none of these explanations is adequate, and in fact the outfields were part of a mature and distinctively south-western agricultural system that probably had rather ancient origins (Fox 1973). An Anglo-Saxon charter of AD 958 granting land at Ayshford and Boehill in east Devon notes at the end of its boundary

Fig. 31.   The curving, parallel earthworks in the fields around Withycombe on
Exmoor show the boundaries of former strip divisions.
Photo: Frances Griffith/DCC, DAP-LC3-SS64, 10th January 1989.

clause that 'here outside the common pasture is the road, from where there are many hills which one may plough' (Finberg 1971; Sawyer 1968 no.653). On Bodmin Moor in Cornwall, archaeological evidence for outfields survives in a few places, and at Bunning's Park in St Neot this could date to before the Norman Conquest (Austin *et al.* 1989). Various maps and documents show that many strip outfield systems were only destroyed quite recently, like the cliff-top example at Rickham Common in East Portlemouth last depicted on the Tithe Map of 1839. Though much of the post-medieval farming of which traces remain as narrow ridge and furrow on Dartmoor was probably undertaken outside of traditional outfield systems (fig. 29), there is archaeological evidence from Devon for outfield agriculture in certain places. Rare examples, like Tinhay Down, Lifton, preserve the remains of common outfields in the form of low lynchets and baulks that once provided the boundaries between the strips (fig. 30).

Surviving open strip fields are rare in the Devon landscape today. The only active one mapped by the Devon HLC is Braunton Great Field. As we have seen, the vestiges of former common outfield strips are visible in grassland at a few other places, as on Tinhay

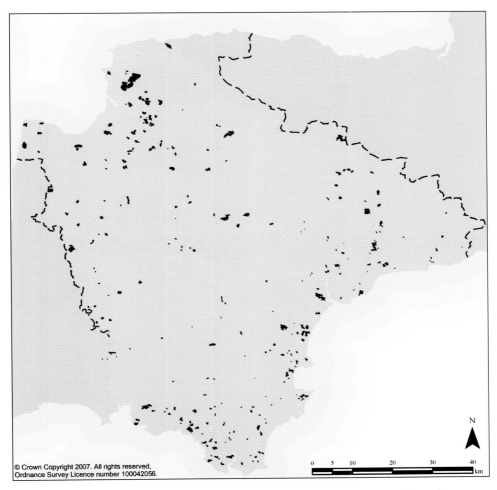

Fig. 36.   Distribution of strip enclosures in Devon, *c.*1890. The olive-coloured area
shows the total area mapped during the Devon HLC project (note that the project excluded
Exmoor National Park). The dashed lines show the county of Devon's land boundaries
with its neighbours. Source: Devon HLC.

two long narrow enclosures are all that remain today of a once extensive area of strips (fig.
35). In 1992, archaeologists identified medieval pottery datable to the 13th or 14th centuries
being eroded from two of the hedgebanks here. The pottery was relatively unweathered,
which implies it had not been broken long when it was incorporated into the boundary
banks. It strongly suggests these strip enclosures were created in the later medieval period,
probably during the 14th century (Devon HER, site no. SS41NE/80). It seems likely that the
vast majority of fields with this characteristic strip enclosure shape were created during the
later Middle Ages, probably between the 12th and 15th centuries.

The distribution of strip enclosures revealed by the HLC mapping shows that at the end
of the 19th century they were most common around large hamlets, villages and small towns
with medieval origins (fig. 36). Some of the most extensive strip field systems surrounded
royal or ecclesiastical manors that had been important sites since Anglo-Saxon times,
like Braunton, Axminster, Kingsteignton and Ottery St Mary. Though the history of their

Fig. 37.   Hardisworthy, Hartland, from the west. A few long, narrow, curving strip enclosures survive to the east of the settlement, but it is clear that the whole field system here had the same origins. Photo: Frances Griffith/DCC, DAP TB10 SS22 Hardisworthy 17th July 1990.

development needs more research, it is quite possible that the large strip fields themselves have also existed since before the Norman Conquest. Others are found around smaller villages and hamlets from the South Hams (as at Holbeton) to the north coast (for example around Milford, Elmscott and many other places in Hartland and the neighbouring parishes: fig. 37).

Enclosures based on Strip Fields

As defined for the purposes of the Devon HLC and this book, medieval strip enclosures are always much longer than they are wide: they were made from either a single strip or a few strips lying side by side. By contrast, most of Devon's late medieval enclosures seem to have been created from larger bundles of strips - they are usually rectangular but with more equal sides than strip enclosures. Nevertheless, both these types of medieval fields share certain important characteristics, all of which are evidence for their origins as strip

Fig. 38. Blegberry, Hartland, looking south. Sinuous field boundaries of medieval origin, showing the 'aratral' curve. The soilmarks of now destroyed boundaries are visible in the ploughed field to the north-west of the hamlet.
Photo: Frances Griffith/DCC, DAP TA7 SS22 Blegberry, 17th July 1990.

fields. Firstly, they normally have sinuous field boundaries, which often show the so-called 'aratral curve' when seen from above or on the map (also known as 'reversed s' or 'reversed j' curves; see Herring 2006a) (fig. 38). It is thought that these curves may reflect the shape of the earlier strips, originally created as the ploughteam swung out in preparation for the turn at the end of the strip (hence 'aratral'). They are widespread in medieval fields all over Britain, being a classic feature of the ridge and furrow landscapes of the Midlands (Hall 1982). There are many blocks of fields with parallel, gently curving boundaries in Devon (figs 39 & 40). Other common features are 'dog-legs' (figs 41 & 42). These kinks in field boundaries either show where blocks of strips once met or else are a sign that a former boundary between two or more fields has been removed. The medieval enclosures south of Leper Fields (Little Torrington) provide some good examples. If we draw back from the individual strip enclosures discussed in the previous section to take a wider view of the landscape, we can see that the larger fields to the south have also been created from blocks of medieval strips (fig. 43).

Whereas strip enclosures generally result from the piecemeal enclosure of one or two strips at a time by individual tenants (Fox 1972), the majority of fields with medieval origins surviving today seem likely to have been created in one of two other ways. Firstly, there

Fig. 39.   Parallel curving blocks of medieval enclosures based
on strip fields at Viveham, East Down. Photo: © getmapping, 2000.

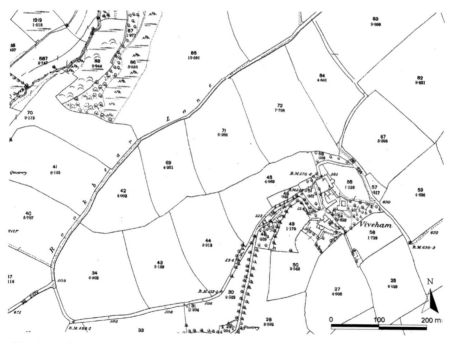

Fig. 40.   Viveham: the same area shown in fig. 39, from the late 19th-century OS 1st edition 1:2,500
map. Map reproduced by kind permission of Landmark. © and database right Crown copyright and
Landmark Information Group Ltd (all rights reserved 2007).

Fig. 41.   Lower Netherton, Haccombe with Combe, on the south side of the Teign estuary, looking north. The photo shows several interesting archaeological and landscape features. First, there are the medieval enclosures based on strip fields, with their curving boundaries and 'dog-legs'. A cropmark dog-leg can be seen in the field to the south of the historic orchard around the settlement. On both sides of the new pipeline which is slicing through the historic boundaries, there are cropmarks of probable prehistoric enclosures. Photo: Frances Griffith/ DCC, DAP MF11 SX87 Netherton, 23rd June 1989.

are cases where an individual farmer had gained ownership or tenancy of a larger block of contiguous strips. This was very common, especially in the 14th and 15th centuries. At this time the population of rural settlements was commonly shrinking and hamlets dwindled to isolated farmsteads in many parts of Devon and Cornwall (Fox 1975; 1983; Herring 2006a). A farmer who had expanded his holding by incorporating land formerly farmed by his neighbours would have been able to enclose bundles of several strips at once. Where his holding stretched across several furlongs that lay next to one another, and where it could all be enclosed in one go, the new fields might form a regular pattern (fig. 44). Secondly, there were blocks of strip fields like the ones at Challacombe that were probably supplied with boundary banks from the beginning. In these cases entire fields – or 'cropping units' – could become 'several' enclosures under the control of one farmer simply by using the existing stock-proof boundaries (Herring 2006a). In either case, the actual cultivation of crops might well have continued in strips, even when the fields had been enclosed. This is suggested, for example, by evidence from early modern pictures like the 1662 etching of Torre Abbey whose background shows many hedged fields subdivided into strips (Gray 2003: 148). Unfortunately, without detailed archaeological evidence, these two processes are very hard

Fig. 42. Dog-legs in curving, originally medieval field boundaries between Blackhorse and the Pin Brook, Sowton. Photo: Sam Turner, July 2006.

to distinguish. Nevertheless, the enclosed fields they created still provide the dominant character of much of Devon and Cornwall's rural landscape today (Herring 2006a).

Harold Fox argued that the enclosure movement that created these small medieval fields and their sinuous boundaries was most common between the 13th and 16th centuries (Fox 1975). Archaeological projects undertaken at places like Brown Willy in Cornwall (Herring 2006b) and Holne Moor on Dartmoor (Fleming & Ralph 1982) have since suggested enclosure might have been underway before it was commonly recorded in documents, but in general Fox's interpretation of the historical evidence still provides a reasonable outline chronology. The later Middle Ages is the most likely period of origin for the majority of Devon's enclosures based on earlier strip fields.

Despite this there are certain exceptions and complicating factors. There are reasons why some types of strip fields were not enclosed until later, as we saw in the case of the common outfields discussed earlier in this chapter. Even when this did not occur until the 17th century, it could lead to fields with sinuous boundaries that look very much like medieval closes. A well-studied example comes from Sowton near Exeter, where Nat Alcock made a detailed study of medieval and early modern maps and documents (Alcock 1975). Here, Sowton Heath and Herring Down were not enclosed until the middle of the 17th century, and yet 18th- and 19th-century maps reveal small fields with curving parallel boundaries typical of enclosed strips (Alcock 1975: 107-10). It is also important to note that the fields around Sowton Barton, enclosed since at least the 16th century, have a much more regular appearance. In this they are similar to many fields in the South Hams, where enclosure of strip fields continued into the later 16th and 17th centuries (Fox 1972: 85-6; 1975). These rather more regular fields are discussed below, but it is worth noting that from at least the 15th century onwards the way new fields looked did not only depend on the date they were enclosed. The pattern of landholding and landuse at the time of enclosure, the social status of the owner or tenant, and the use intended for the fields could be just as important. This highlights the importance of detailed local study, and the HLC maps, which present a generalised picture with rather coarse chronological definition, should not be used as a proxy for this kind of ground-level research.

In some ways the removal of open strip fields through late medieval enclosure did

0   100   200   300   400   500 metres   N

Fig. 43.   Medieval enclosures south of Leper Fields, Little Torrington. Photo: © getmapping, 2000.

revolutionise the landscape. The old rights over strips in Devon's small communal fields were never as complicated as in the Midlands and elsewhere. As they were extinguished, more and more owners and tenants held their land 'in severalty' (i.e. privately). As Finberg argued,

> . . . within their several enclosures both lord and tenants could do as they pleased.
>
> (Finberg 1951: 103).

These physical changes in the landscape were also linked to changes in regional economies and the ways the (much reduced) rural populations made their livings (Fox 1989, 1995; Dyer 1997). In other ways, though, much remained the same as it had been for centuries. As Harold Fox has argued, the end of communal strip field agriculture did not necessarily mean the old farming regimes were changed beyond recognition (Fox 1991b: 309). Just as Devon and Cornwall had different field systems to the Midland counties, they also had different patterns of crop rotation in the Middle Ages. We have already considered the extreme example of the outfield arable, which might be cultivated at up to 50-year intervals, and there were longer rotations in south-western infields too than in the Midlands. Documentary sources show that a system now known as 'convertible husbandry' was in

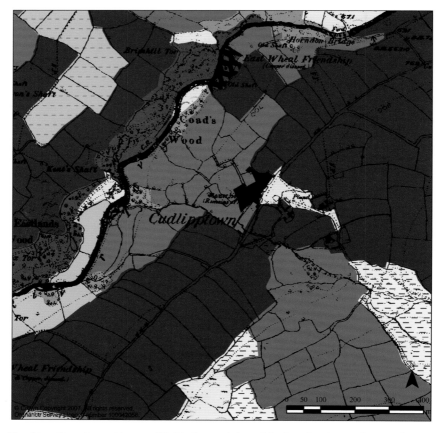

Fig. 44.   Regular patterns of fields formed from blocks of strips to the south-west
and north-east of Cudlipptown, Peter Tavy. The late 19th century HLC is
displayed against the OS 1st edition 1:10,560 map. Map reproduced by kind
permission of Landmark. © and database right Crown copyright and Landmark
Information Group Ltd (all rights reserved 2007).

operation by at least the 13th century. Ralph Fyfe, a specialist in understanding ancient
environments based on the evidence of buried plant pollen, has recently suggested that the
system may have its origins as early as the eighth century, using data from mid-Devon. If
so convertible husbandry would have begun as part of the major landscape reorganisation
that took place in the early Middle Ages, when the foundations of the medieval (and
modern) settlement pattern were laid (Fyfe 2006). In this system there would be a large
number of fields or cropping units around a farm or hamlet. At any time most of the fields
would be under grass, with a few under arable crops. These were prepared for cultivation by
ploughing and then burning the grassy turf, whose ashes were subsequently spread across
the field (Herring 2006a). Each field could be kept under arable for a few years before being
returned to pasture, and convertible husbandry could be practised just as easily in enclosed
fields as in open strip fields. This fact, together with the ubiquity of long grass leys, must have
made it easier for medieval farmers to enclose their fields in Devon. Although convertible
husbandry was not unique to the county or even to the South West, it was known by the 16th
century as 'Denshiring' or Devonshiring, and in the post-medieval period came to influence
agricultural practice across much of England.

The widespread practice of convertible husbandry also helps to explain one other peculiarity of Devon's historic landscape. Unlike much of Midland England, archaeological evidence for ridge and furrow is rather rare in Devon. In some counties, like Norfolk, it is possible that the medieval agricultural regime was such that very little ridge and furrow was ever created (Williamson 2003). This may also have been the case in parts of Devon, and as we have already seen in open fields like Braunton the boundaries between strips were marked only by low baulks of earth. These would presumably have been rather easier to erase when the field came into the hands of a single farmer than the great ridges that characterise medieval farming in Northamptonshire or Northumberland. Nevertheless, there was medieval ridge and furrow in parts of Devon, as we know from the physical

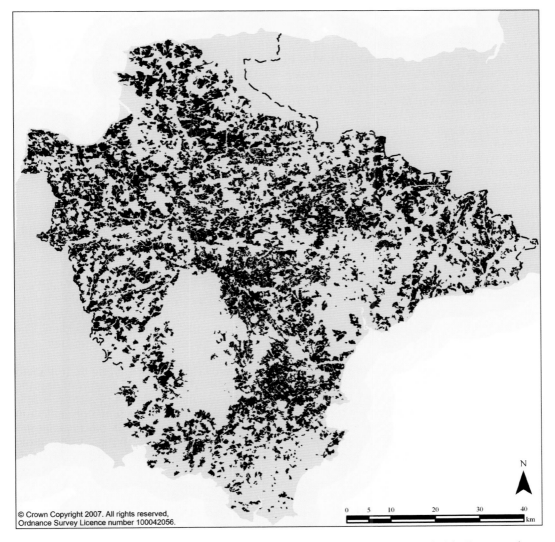

Fig. 45. The distribution of fields with origins as 'medieval fields based on strips' in Devon today. This map does not show 'barton fields' (see fig. 54) or medieval fields with significant post-medieval alterations (fig. 63), though these types are also commonly based on medieval strip fields. Source: Devon HLC.

evidence that has survived at places like Houndtor (Manaton) and Rackenford Moor (Brandon 1979). The fact that most of it now lies on the moors, which have been cultivated only sporadically since medieval times, hints that the reason so little ridge and furrow survives elsewhere in Devon is because it has been destroyed by post-medieval and modern farming. As each field within a farm's rotation would have been ploughed regularly (if only once or twice every decade), both ridges and baulks between strips would now have been erased. The archaeological evidence hints that this is indeed what has happened, and faint traces of possible ridge and furrow have been detected in Devon fields from both air photographs and geophysical survey. For example, at Charlestown Barton (Charles) on the edge of Exmoor, geophysical survey suggests the present fields around the Barton replaced earlier ridge and furrow cultivation on a different alignment (Humphreys 2004).

Medieval enclosures based on strip fields are the most common landscape character type in Devon. They occur in every parish in the county, and in many they still cover by far the greatest proportion of the land. Fields of this type occupied around 32% of the total land area in 1890 (fig. 45), and over 60% of them have remained substantially unchanged by the developments of the 20th century. In the area to the south-east of Dartmoor between Ashburton and Torbay, for example, most fields are of this type. Nevertheless, their distribution and density does vary from region to region, and the HLC model of late 19th-century Devon shows that this is not just due to the vagaries of 20th-century field boundary removal. In the coastal belt of the South Hams, for example, there are far smaller areas of this character type than we might expect. This distribution owes a great deal to medieval and early modern farming practice, and to the dates when enclosure took place. Regional differences in the distributions of various character types are considered again in Chapter 5.

Other Medieval Enclosures

We cannot claim that all Devon's enclosures with medieval origins were once arable fields, and some show no signs of strip field farming. It is often rather hard to tell exactly what the original function of irregular fields might have been, and the evidence suggests a range of different uses. Most fields with really irregular shapes have been included in this category for the Devon HLC, so I am using it here to stand for several different types of land use that can be very hard to distinguish and date without detailed archaeological and historical work. Often we can make guesses about the original use from the context; so for example little closes round a farmstead will probably have been small paddocks and gardens. The most common types of fields included in the category of 'Other Medieval Enclosures' are:

i. Large enclosures made up of medieval demesne fields (land held directly by a manor) which were subsequently subdivided in the late- and/or early post-medieval periods, typically between the 14th and 17th centuries. Unlike the 'barton fields' discussed below, the irregular field boundaries of this type do not necessarily show evidence of enclosure from strips in the form of regular curving boundaries (with s- or j-curves). Good examples are the former fields of Newenham Abbey near Axminster, which in the Middle Ages were apparently without major subdivisions (Fox 1972). In the 17th century, several of the demesne fields became farms in their own right after they were split into four or more enclosures, for example Balles Close and Slymelake Close (fig. 46).

ii. Irregular medieval enclosures like the ones at Houndtor (Brandon 1979). Really irregular fields sometimes seem to have been created by making clearances from woodland, heath or moorland in the late medieval and early post-medieval periods. Documents from Axminster parish suggest that enclosure of woodland and rough ground commenced in the later 13th century and continued into the 16th. In particular, there are 16th-century records of enclosure from the north-western part of the parish at Cox Wood, Fawsmoor

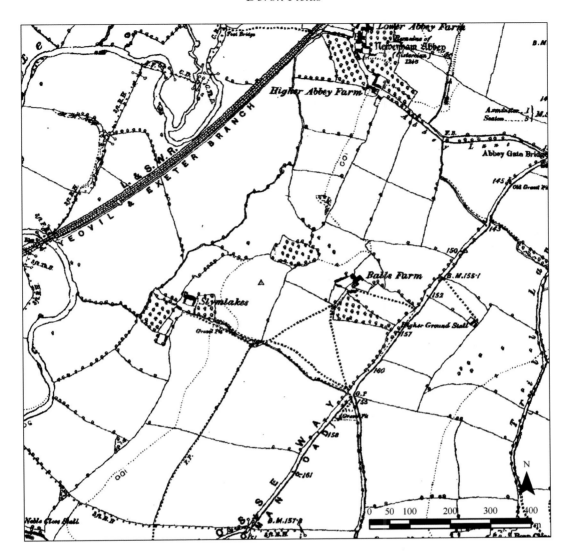

Fig. 46.   Farms established in the former medieval fields of Balles Close and Slymelake Close near Axminster. OS 1st edition 1:10,560 map. Map reproduced by kind permission of Landmark. © and database right Crown copyright and Landmark Information Group Ltd (all rights reserved 2007).

and Symonds Down (fig. 47). Whitcombe Wood was 'half felled' by 1574, and completely enclosed 'by uniform consent' of tenants by 1630. Whilst fields like these were often irregular in form, it is important to remember that they might still have been farmed in strips. The evidence from Houndtor clearly shows that medieval strip field farming did sometimes occur in enclosures with highly irregular shapes. If it was not for the fact that strip divisions have been preserved as earthworks for archaeologists to record, it is highly unlikely that strip field farming would have been identified here based on just the shape of the fields. These fields were probably provided with substantial boundaries from the outset, perhaps to limit damage from the many thousands of grazing animals who were brought up

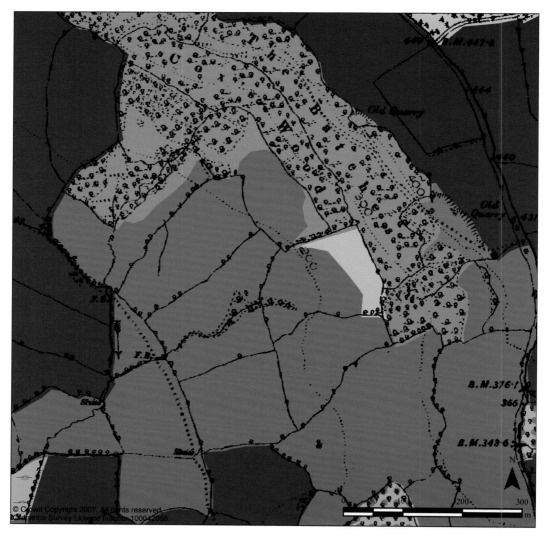

Fig. 47.   Enclosures from woodland and rough ground at Cox Wood, Axminster (see Fox 1972).
The late 19th century HLC is drawn against the OS 1st edition 1:10,560 map, 1891.
Map reproduced by kind permission of Landmark. © and database right Crown copyright
and Landmark Information Group Ltd (all rights reserved 2007).

onto Dartmoor for the summer pastures (Fox 1994). It is worth bearing in mind that many
other highly irregular medieval enclosures are likely to have contained strip fields – they
would have been part of the normal farming pattern of medieval Devon.

iii. Meadow (other than watermeadows) and pasture land that was not part of the
convertible husbandry regime. Such fields often occur along the course of streams; a
good example can be seen in fig. 31. Whilst this probably always formed a relatively small
proportion of the total land area, medieval documents show it was nonetheless present
in many areas (e.g. Fox 1975: 185; 1991a: 153-4). The area of such land fluctuated during

58

Fig. 48. Small enclosures and paddocks around the medieval settlement at Houndtor, Manaton. Photo: Frances Griffith/DCC, DAP EO3 Houndtor, 17th March 1985.

the Middle Ages and after, and it may be that much of it was made up of fields that were ploughed for arable sometimes and not at other times. The Devon HLC certainly does not map as much land as 'Other Medieval Enclosures' as Harold Fox has identified as meadow and pasture from the medieval records. This is probably because many such fields had been used for arable land at one time or another, and so look today very much like fields that were part of the convertible husbandry system.

iv. The miscellaneous paddocks and closes that often occur around medieval farmsteads, for example the Sourton Down enclosure or the little yards around the houses at Houndtor (fig. 48). (Weddell & Reed 1997). These are commonly small and rather irregular, and are normally found in close association with medieval settlements. In fact, the remains of such enclosures commonly provide a good indication of deserted medieval sites in Devon (fig. 49).

These fields have mostly been included in this historic landscape character type for a practical reason: they all share certain characteristics that can make them hard to distinguish today. Most importantly, they all have fairly sinuous, irregular boundaries that do not seem to follow the edges of former strips, perhaps the most important aspect of their

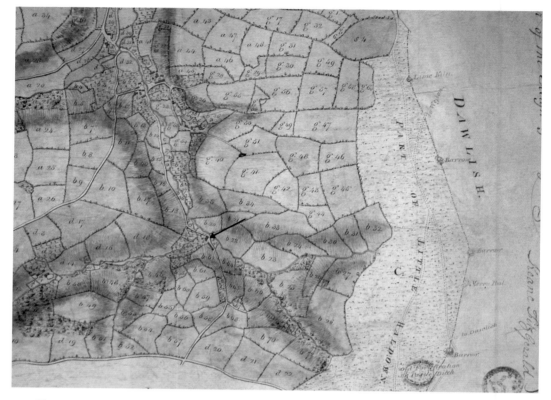

Fig. 49.   An estate map of the late 1820s showing (arrowed) the settlement of Seacombe or
Sackham on the slopes of Little Haldon, which was deserted by the 1890s.
Devon Record Office, DRO 484M-T3-20
(by kind permission of Sir Geoffrey Newman).

character in the modern landscape. Dating the creation of these fields based on their shapes
is particularly tricky because of their diverse origins. Some, like the fields at Houndtor, are
certainly medieval; others are later, like the sub-divisions of Newenham Abbey's demesne
fields. Unfortunately, these historical problems are not easy to resolve without detailed
research, which highlights once again the value of further detailed local studies.

FIELDS WITH POST-MEDIEVAL ORIGINS

Barton fields

From the 15th century onwards, we can detect certain changes in the countryside that have
been linked to an increased focus on production for external markets and the drive to make
more and more profit from the land (Turner, forthcoming). Historians argue that different
regions were developing their own distinctive economies around this time. Rising rents
were linked to the appreciation that land itself was a commodity, and there was a growing
awareness of the financial benefits of using new agricultural techniques. Such links are
explicitly recognised by contemporary agricultural writers like Fitzherbert, whose farming
handbook of 1523 starts with the words:

Here begynneth a ryght frutefull mater: and hath to name *the boke of surveyeng and improvmentes.*

Like most medieval enclosures, many of the closes created between the 15th and 17th centuries were based on medieval strip fields that had come into the possession of a single landowner. These new fields tended to be increasingly regular and to impose new divisions on the landscape rather than just follow the lines established by earlier farmers. We can identify them in today's landscape by a mixture of slightly sinuous hedgebanks (particularly in cases where some evidence survives of 'aratral' curves), together with some almost straight boundaries; the fields are also often large by south-western standards (fig. 50). In Cornwall, they have been given the name 'Barton fields' because they often occur around farms with 'Barton' place-names (Herring 1998; and see further below); for convenience, I have used the same term in this book.

After examining the written sources for the dates when different parts of medieval Devon were enclosed, Harold Fox drew attention to the contrast between the fields of Axminster and the later enclosures in the South Hams around Stoke Fleming and Slapton (Fox 1972; 1975). In this fertile part of south Devon the field patterns are much more regular, with large enclosures stretching out from the villages towards the parish boundaries (fig. 51). Many are clearly based on former cropping units in once common strip fields, with parallel, slightly curving boundaries marking the general alignment of former furlongs. Similar pattens are also common in the Exe valley. For example, at Bishop's Clyst the fields of the manorial demesne were divided into smallish, regular closes during the 16th and 17th centuries and leased out for a profit to tenant farmers (fig. 52). Until their destruction during recent redevelopment, vestiges of ridge and furrow cultivation may have survived here (Alcock 1975). It seems likely that all these examples show places where medieval landscapes

Fig. 50.   Typical barton fields around Straightgate Farm, Ottery St Mary.
Photo: Sam Turner, November 2005.

Fig. 51.   Barton fields around Slapton. OS 1st edition 1:10,560 map, 1889–90.
Map reproduced by kind permission of Landmark. © and database right Crown copyright
and Landmark Information Group Ltd (all rights reserved 2007).

of open arable fields were transformed into stock-rearing enclosures, better suited to generating a profit in the changing economy of the early modern period. Nevertheless, the greatest concentration of these fields is found in south and mid Devon and the lower Exe valley, areas that are traditionally associated with arable farming. The presence of many barton-type fields in these regions is probably due to the lateness of enclosure here: the documents tell us that some places still had open field arable as late as the 17th century, for example South Huish and Galmpton (Fox 1975: 187, n.3).

In the written sources, we can sometimes see alterations in the late medieval fieldscape being undertaken by specific landowners (Turner, forthcoming). At both Buckfastleigh and Crediton, for example, a man named Sir Thomas Dennis acquired land from the church

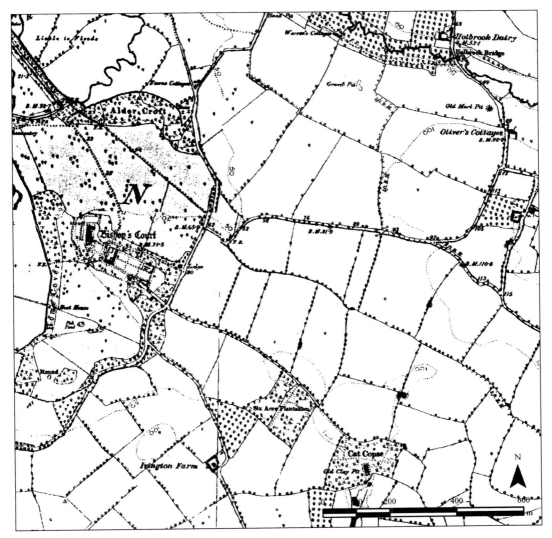

Fig. 52. Barton fields in the Exe valley: Bishop's Clyst as depicted on the OS 1st edition 1:10,560 map, 1890. Map reproduced by kind permission of Landmark. © and database right Crown copyright and Landmark Information Group Ltd (all rights reserved 2007).

after the dissolution of the monasteries under Henry VIII. He seems to have created new, regular enclosures on the land he had gained, probably in order to maximise rents from his tenants. The former deerpark at Crediton Great Park was divided into a patchwork of farms with many regular fields. At Buckfastleigh, fields around Holy Trinity church that formerly belonged to Buckfast Abbey were divided into smaller, more regular enclosures in the 1540s (fig. 54). In both places the form of these regular fields contrasts with the sinuous medieval enclosures of neighbouring farms.

Such changes were sometimes contentious. Sarah Child's research on the hamlet of Backstone in Rackenford shows how the common arable fields of a small hamlet were divided into separate enclosures during the 16th century, and how this led to a bitter dispute

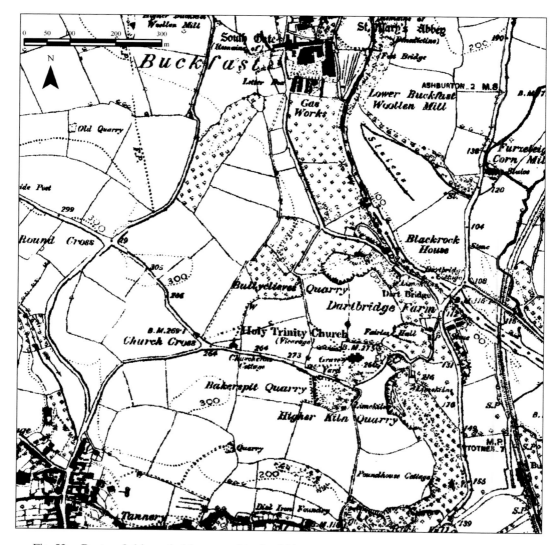

Fig. 53. Barton fields probably created in the 16th century around the church of Holy Trinity, Buckfastleigh. Orchards and quarries also surround the limestone hill on which the church stands. OS 1st edition 1:10,560 map, 1889-91. Map reproduced by kind permission of Landmark.
© and database right Crown copyright and Landmark Information Group Ltd
(all rights reserved 2007). (See also fig. 98).

between the hamlet's two farmers in the 17th (Child 2001). Indeed, it was not just the demesne land of major lords that witnessed changes at this time; others from merchants and lawyers to the lords of small manors and the descendants of medieval freeholders were also busy re-organising their land. Power to alter and improve the enclosed fields could have emphasised the growing status of such people, and we might suspect that disputes between them were linked not only to income but also to their local prestige.

A glance at the map of Devon and Cornwall reveals that there are many farms whose names include the word 'Barton'. H.P.R. Finberg noticed that from the 14th century

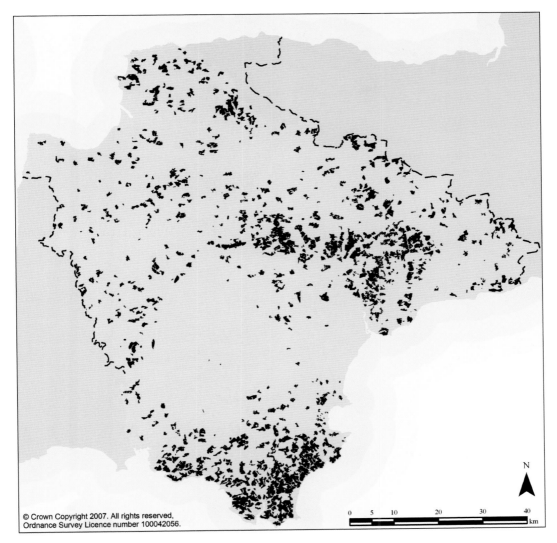

Fig. 54.   Distribution of barton fields in Devon, *c.*1890. Source: Devon HLC.

onwards it was used to signify the home farm of a manor, and suggested that barton '…may first have acquired this meaning through deliberate withdrawal of the magnates [from the open fields with intermixed strips] into ring-fenced manor farms' (Finberg 1951: 49). It was clearly linked, therefore, to the creation of new field types from this time. Around the end of the 16th century, the Cornish scholar and antiquary Richard Carew noted that

> that part of the demesne which appertaineth to the lord's dwelling-house they call his barton, or berton (Carew 1953: 122).

As time went by, the name was increasingly applied to the farms of other people who had also consolidated their holdings into compact blocks of land. By the 17th or 18th centuries,

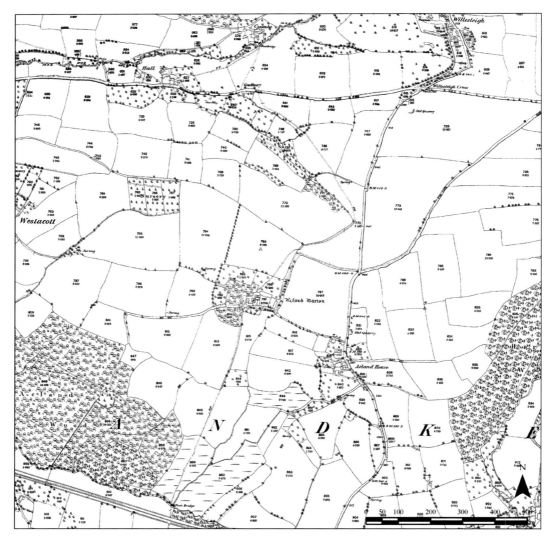

Fig. 55. One of Hoskins' bartons: Acland Barton, near Barnstaple. 1st edn OS 1:2,500 map, 1888–90. Map reproduced by kind permission of Landmark. © and database right Crown copyright and Landmark Information Group Ltd (all rights reserved 2007).

some parishes and manors contained several farms with 'barton' names, and the HLC maps reveal that barton-type fields can be found in many Devon parishes (fig. 54).

The great Devon historian W.G. Hoskins pointed out that many of the barton names are associated with farms where late medieval and early modern farmhouses survive. He suggested the names were associated with a major phase of rebuilding (Hoskins 1966). Both the Cornwall and Devon farms with 'barton' names are often associated with a characteristically regular arrangement of fields. Whilst such fields are not laid out with perfectly surveyed straight boundaries like later post-medieval enclosures, they are normally larger and almost always more regular than those in surrounding holdings. Regular fields like these surround all the farms in Devon with barton-names discussed by Hoskins: at

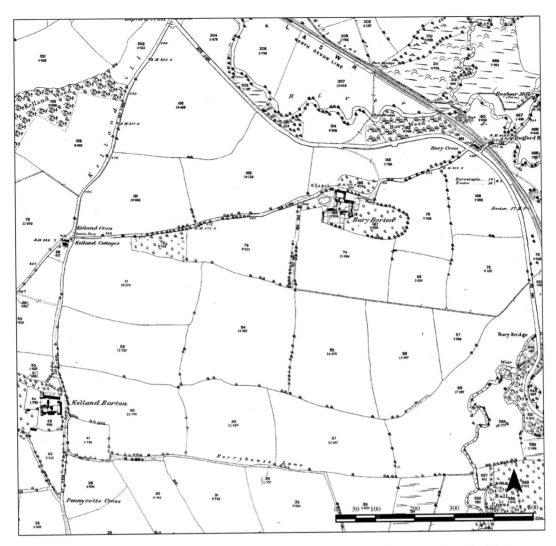

Fig. 56. Bury Barton, Lapford. 1st edn OS 1:2,500 map, 1889. Map reproduced by kind permission of Landmark. © and database right Crown copyright and Landmark Information Group Ltd (all rights reserved 2007).

Acland Barton (Landkey), Bury Barton (Lapford), Colleton Barton (Chulmleigh), Honiton Barton (South Molton), Shapcott Barton (Knowstone), Rashleigh Barton (Wembworthy), Upcott Barton (Cheriton Fitzpaine) and Westcott Barton (Marwood) (figs 55-57).

We should note, however, that not all new fields created between the 15th and 17th centuries are shaped like the large and regular barton fields. Enclosures cut from woodland and heath, like the ones round the edges of Axminster parish or the fields of ring-fence farms on Bodmin Moor, had much more in common with their medieval predecessors (Herring 1986). The chronological overlap shows us two important things: firstly, it was a deliberate choice to make regular barton fields, which we might interpret as a way for landowners to show prestige; secondly, it is sometimes hard to link the shape of fields to the date of their

Fig. 57.   Rashleigh Barton, Wembworthy, its relatively regular fields contrasting
clearly with those of its neighbours. 1st edn OS 1:10,560 map, 1890–91. Map reproduced by kind
permission of Landmark. © and database right Crown copyright and Landmark
Information Group Ltd (all rights reserved 2007).

enclosure. This is particularly the case during the late medieval and early modern periods, when field shape seems to have as much to do with the processes of enclosure and the type of people undertaking it as the date the fields were made.

However, where it is possible to map barton fields we can be reasonably sure that they had their origins between the 15th and 17th centuries, and that they were linked to changing agricultural practices by their owners. It is also very likely that most were created out of former strip fields (fig. 58).

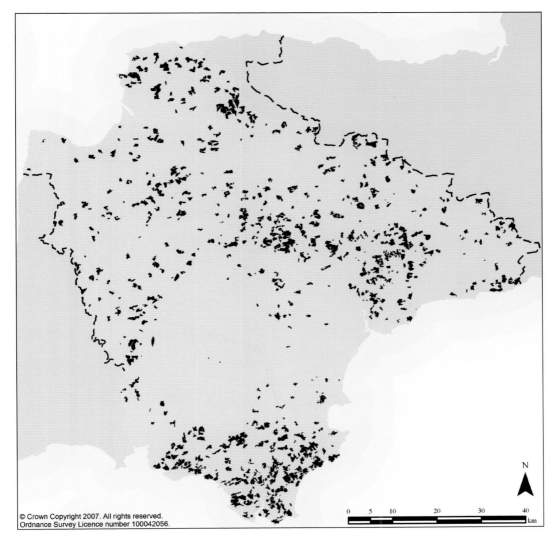

Fig. 58. Distribution of barton fields in Devon, *c.*2000. Many barton field systems suffered considerably from boundary removal during the 20th century.

Post-medieval enclosures

During the 17th and 18th centuries, the fashion for increasingly regular field patterns that began to emerge in the later Middle Ages spread throughout rural society. By about 1800, the great majority of new field boundaries created in Devon (and elsewhere in England) were as straight as rulers. For this reason they are relatively easy for us to detect, both in the landscape and on the map.

By comparison with the upheavals in Midland England, the 'ancient countryside' of the West Country seems to have suffered relatively few changes in the last few centuries, as we saw in Chapter 1 (Rackham 1986: 5).

This view of the south-western landscape as largely unchanged since the end of the Middle Ages has also been endorsed by historians like W.G. Hoskins, who wrote in his great book *Devon* that:

> It is in [the] generations between 1150 and 1350 that the characteristic Devonian landscape was born: the lanes, the small irregular fields, the great hedge-banks, the isolated farmstead at the end of the track, and the little parish church . . . By

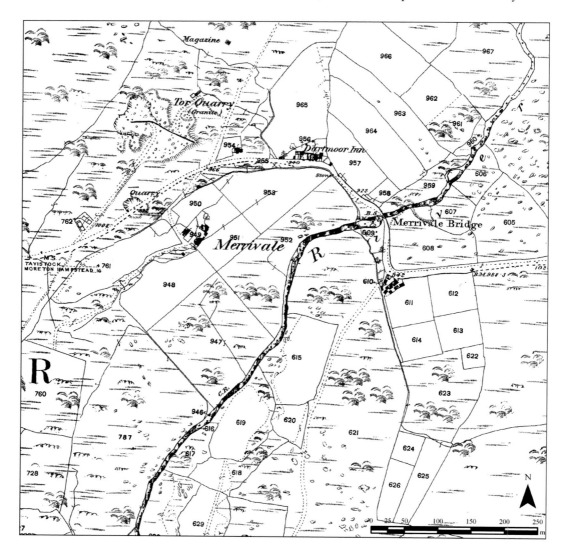

Fig. 59.   Straight-sided post-medieval fields at Merrivale. Earlier enclosures are visible to the north of the settlement. 1st edn OS 1:2,500 map, 1884–85. Map reproduced by kind permission of Landmark. © and database right Crown copyright and Landmark Information Group Ltd (all rights reserved 2007).

1350 nearly every name was written on the map of Devon, nearly every line was drawn.

(Hoskins 1954: 72-2).

As we saw in the section on fields with medieval origins, these arguments are true in many ways: much of the fabric of today's rural landscape has its roots in the Middle Ages. But it is not correct to say that little has changed in the Devon countryside since 1700. In fact, the agricultural revolutions of the 18th, 19th and 20th centuries have left indelible marks on the farming landscape, some of which have altered the character of certain regions almost

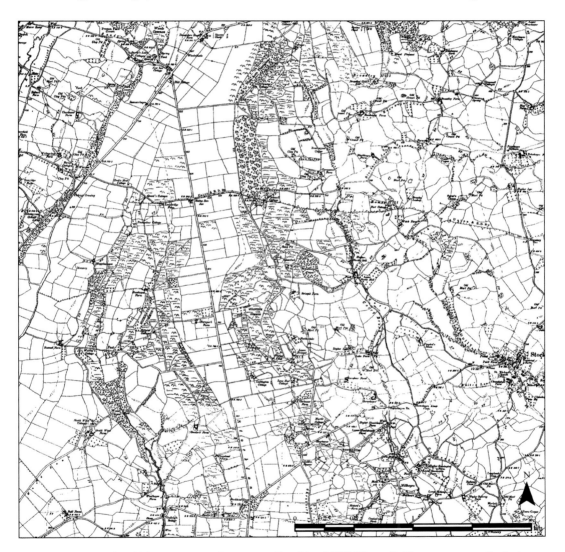

Fig. 60. Regular 19th-century enclosures on Stockland Hill. These fields contrast particularly strongly with the sinuous medieval fields in the adjacent valleys. 1st edn OS 1:10,560 map, first revision, 1904–05. Map reproduced by kind permission of Landmark. © and database right Crown copyright and Landmark Information Group Ltd (all rights reserved 2007).

Fig. 61. A view across the northern end of Stockland Hill, from the east. Photo: Frances Griffith/DCC, Devon HER, ST20SW

Fig. 62. The southern part of Stockland Hill, from the east. Prehistoric enclosures are visible at Stockland Great Castle (irregular feature with tall trees, centre left) and Stockland Little Castle (the almost circular field, centre right). The regular grid of post-medieval fields contrasts sharply with both the prehistoric enclosures and the medieval fields lower down the hillsides. Photo: Frances Griffith/DCC, 21st March 1988.

beyond recognition. 20th-century trajectories of change are considered below, and some of the effects of post-medieval industry (like the boom in mining) are discussed in the following chapter. In this section, I will look briefly at the many new fields and alterations to old fields made in the 18th and 19th centuries.

These fields with post-medieval historic character can be divided into two main categories: enclosures of former rough ground, and enclosures within the existing medieval fieldscape. I will begin with the rough ground – the moorland, heathland, and rough pasture – which is considered as a historic landscape type in its own right in the next chapter. As discussed there, the HLC mapping reveals that rough ground was much more widespread in Devon before the enclosures of the 18th and 19th centuries.

From the second half of the 18th century, farms with ruler-straight, surveyed field boundaries became increasingly common on the south-western moors. At first, contemporary observers were not convinced about the merits of bringing such wild land under the plough, and writers like William Marshall doubted they would be profitable (1796b, 31-2). Ambitious developers pressed on with their schemes and created farms like Sir Thomas Tyrwhitt's 706-acre Tor Royal out of land that had previously been rough moorland (Fletcher & Dunn 1999). The fact that much of this remained uncultivated was apparently no deterrent for later developers like the Knight family, who acquired and attempted to improve great areas of Exmoor from 1818 onwards (Orwin *et al.* 1997; Riley & Wilson-North 2001). Even when it became clear to them twenty years later that arable farming was not going to be profitable, huge investments were still made to boost livestock production. These large-scale post-medieval 'improvements' radically altered the appearance of many of Devon's high moorland areas.

The enterprises of less wealthy men and women also had profound effects on the south-western landscape at this time. By tradition, the tenants of ancient moorland farms on Dartmoor had been entitled to enclose small 'newtakes' from the moors since the Middle Ages. Towards the end of the 18th century the Duchy of Cornwall, who owned the land, realised how vigorously they were abusing their ancient rights and forebade the practice (Havinden & Wilkinson 1970; Somers Cocks 1970). This failed to stop the process of enclosure, however, and energetic efforts to increase the amount of land used for agriculture continued well into the first decades of the 19th century. Smallholders, who were often industrial workers engaged in mining or similar industries, carved out little farms and fields from the uplands which they bounded with straight, modern drystone walls. Such settlements are particularly common in mid and west Cornwall, where thousands of acres of rough ground were first enclosed at this time. They also came to Devon's moors, and the fields of places like Merrivale bear witness to their endeavours (fig. 59). Such enclosures may have become less common as the 19th century wore on, but even so they continued right into the early 20th century at places like South Zeal on the north-east edge of Dartmoor.

Away from the moors, the effects of post-medieval enclosure were perhaps even more profound and long-lasting. Many significant areas of heathland and rough grazing survived in Devon into the 18th and 19th centuries, and vast acreages were enclosed with new regular boundaries after about 1750. Regular fields in many places illustrate this; an excellent example is Stockland Hill in east Devon (fig. 60). The grid pattern of fields on the ridgetop here was created after a parliamentary enclosure act of 1864; their dead-straight boundaries only waver where they meet the ancient tree-clad earthworks of Stockland Great Camp, an irregularly-shaped settlement enclosure of the first millennium BC (figs 61 & 62). Other areas of similar post-medieval enclosures occur all over the county. They are most common in the north and west, where the greatest area of rough ground had been, but they are also to be found in fertile arable zones like the South Hams. Blackdown in Loddiswell was only enclosed in the mid-19th century, along with patches of rough grazing in the neighbouring parishes of Modbury, Aveton Gifford and Moreleigh. The cliff-top grazing and outfield was also enclosed in many places, as at Chivelstone and East Portlemouth, where the former strip field at Rickham Common was split into four regular closes. Much rough ground enclosed in this way had formerly been large, coherent open blocks. However, the process also affected more localised patches of rough grazing that lay intermixed between the medieval fields or along the steep sides and bottoms of coombes and river valleys (Turner 2004). Thanks to the enlargement of individual holdings that took hold from the later medieval period, such areas were often controlled by a single farmer, so records of their enclosure do not often survive. The HLC shows patches of regular post-medieval enclosures all over Devon; in the late 19th century, post-medieval fields still in agricultural use made up as much as 16% of the total area covered by this study.

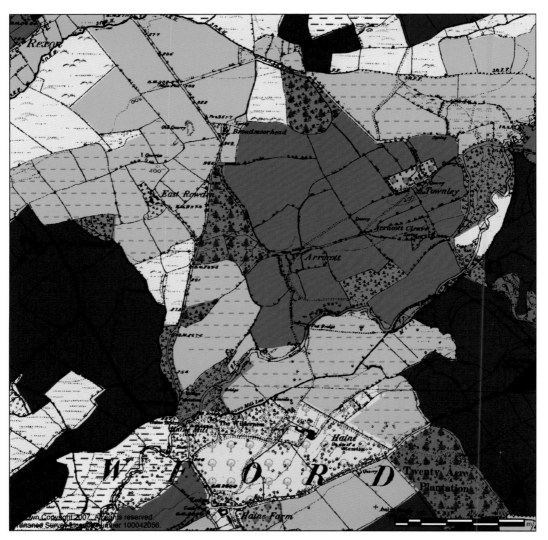

Fig. 63.   Straight post-medieval boundaries inserted into medieval fields around Arracott, East Rowden and Haine, Stowford. The HLC of the landscape c. 1890 is displayed against 1st edn OS 1:10,560 map, 1887-93. Map reproduced by kind permission of Landmark. © and database right Crown copyright and Landmark Information Group Ltd (all rights reserved 2007).

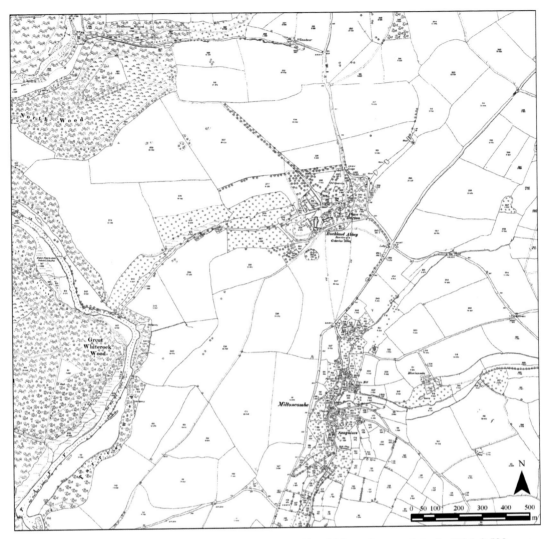

Fig. 64. The landscape around Buckland Abbey, Buckland Monachorum. 1st edn OS 1:2,500 map, 1867–85. Map reproduced by kind permission of Landmark. © and database right Crown copyright and Landmark Information Group Ltd (all rights reserved 2007).

The majority of these new enclosures were created during a period of agricultural expansion and rising prices in the late 18th and early 19th centuries. Some of these fields never proved profitable, particularly on the high moors. Others were sown with crops in the early 19th century, but it seems the farming recession from the 1870s onwards seriously affected their viability. Especially in north-west Devon, many had reverted to rough ground by the end of the 19th century. Even so, the creation of new boundaries and the subsoiling and draining that went hand-in-hand with improvement has had a massive impact on the character of Devon's historic landscape ever since.

Finally, farmers were not just altering the layout and use of rough grazing grounds in the post-medieval period. There were also significant changes afoot within the old medieval enclosures. In the later 19th century, this activity increasingly took the form of removing hedgebanks on the grounds that they impeded modern farming techniques, but until the 1840s it seems just as likely to have involved building new boundaries. In the last decade of the 18th century, the agricultural writer William Marshall still saw the value in Devon's great hedgebanks for shelter, fodder and firewood (1796a: 67-9). In fact, early modern documents refer to the subdivision of existing medieval fields in the South West to create smaller closes (Fox and Padel 1998), and new post-medieval boundaries can often be spotted on the map as ruler-straight lines amidst generally sinuous closes. They are particularly common in parts of north and west Devon like the parishes of Rackenford and Lewtrenchard (fig. 63). A good example can be found in the fields around Place Barton (Buckland Monachorum) in the Tamar valley, the medieval site of Buckland Abbey and home to William Marshall himself during the 18th century (fig. 64). In some places, the fields of entire farms were reorganised more than once: at Aller Barton near Dawlish, for example, the post-medieval fields shown on an estate map of 1827 were remodelled once again during the 19th century.

THE 20TH CENTURY

In a few places, the enclosure of downland or moorland continued into the early decades of the 20th century. Such fields can sometimes be identified by their barbed wire fences and their location on the edges of the rough ground. These changes continued developments that had begun in the post-medieval period, but it was not until after World War II that the agricultural innovations of the modern era had their greatest impact.

In rural Devon, we can identify several trends since this time. Firstly, a significant acreage has witnessed changes in land use. These can be clearly identified by comparing the HLC of the late 19th century with the modern characterisation. The destruction of orchards, the conversion of valley-bottom pasture to arable or improved grassland, and the ploughing up of many

Fig. 65.   Recent wire fences subdividing a field in the Dart valley. Photo: Sam Turner, July 2006.

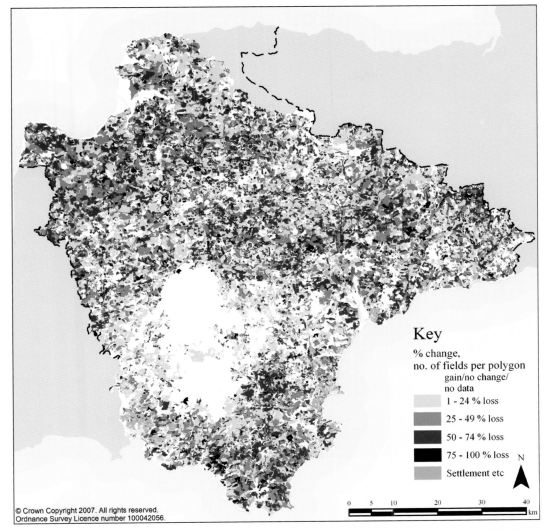

Key

% change,
no. of fields per polygon
gain/no change/
no data

1 - 24 % loss

25 - 49 % loss

50 - 74 % loss

75 - 100 % loss

Settlement etc

Fig. 66. The image represents boundary loss in the 20th century based on the Devon HLC data. It shows the percentage change in the number of fields in each polygon over the last 100 years. Grey shows settlements and industrial areas. The destruction of field boundaries has affected some areas particularly badly, for example the South Hams, north-west Devon, and parts of the Exe and Culm valleys in east Devon.

remaining small areas of rough ground are all very common (these trends are discussed futher in Chapter 4).

Secondly, new field boundaries have been inserted into earlier enclosures to create patterns of small, regular fields. This process is particularly common around major towns like Plymouth and Exeter, where these small paddocks are often used by people living in the towns to keep horses for recreational purposes. Elsewhere, some farmers have preferred the flexibility of the wire fence to the immovable mass of the Devon hedgebank, and have replaced traditional boundaries with temporary ones that can easily be altered to suit changing priorities (fig. 65).

Fig. 67.   Modern fields in the Exe valley. Nether Exe Barton, Nether Exe, looking north.
Photo: Frances Griffith/DCC, 6th July 1984, Devon HER.

By far the most significant modern change is the removal of old hedgebanks to create ever larger fields. It is true that this had begun a hundred years earlier: by the 1840s, agricultural improvers were exhorting Devon's farmers to remove field boundaries in the interests of economy, and research published in the 1930s suggests a considerable response in some areas (Grant 1845; Dymond 1856; Long 1935). Nevertheless, there had probably been relatively little destruction of field boundaries between the 1870s and the 1930s, since arable farming was in decline during this period (Gilg 1999: 308; Overton 2006: 121-3). It was not until after the Second World War that major change began with government schemes to encourage modernisation and mechanisation. It is estimated that a staggering 20,000 km of Devon hedges have been destroyed since 1945 (DCC 2005). This loss is clearly reflected in the HLC data, which shows 'modern fields' covering vast swathes of territory. Although the destruction of individual hedges was not recorded as part of the HLC project, I did note how many fields there were in each polygon in 1890 and how many there are today; comparing the two allows us to represent field boundary loss using the GIS (fig. 66). I described the character of an area as 'modern' whenever there were half as many fields (or less) today than there were a hundred years ago. In many places, particularly on rich arable land like the lower-lying stretches of the Exe valley, this field boundary destruction has radically altered the character of the modern landscape (fig. 67). In other places the effects have been less drastic: the hedgebanks and other boundaries that survive are often still ancient, so preserving the essential aspects of the ancient countryside.

The outlook for Devon's hedges is perhaps better now than at any time in the last 200 years. Devon County Council estimates that there are at least 53,000 km of traditional boundaries surviving, and they are increasingly being valued by diverse groups from farmers to ecologists. New regulations are in place to protect hedgerows, and countryside management schemes like Entry Level Stewardship and Higher Level Stewardship actively reward landowners for looking after them sympathetically. Nevertheless, hedges are still being lost either through deliberate removal or neglect; as discussed in Chapter 6, the HLC can help target areas for conservation and restoration.

CONCLUSION

By around 1900, fields whose origins lay in the medieval and post-medieval periods covered around 67% of the total area of Devon studied for the HLC project. There can be no question that the farmers who made and maintained these fields have had a greater impact on Devon's modern landscape than any other single group of people. Even so, over 30% of the county was dedicated to other ways of using the land, for example as rough grazing ground and woodland, watermeadows and orchards. I will consider the most important of these land uses in the next chapter.

CHAPTER 4

MOORS AND MINES, WOODS AND WATERMEADOWS: OTHER HISTORIC LAND USES

INTRODUCTION

By the end of the Middle Ages, fields and farms were laid out across most of the Devon landscape. Even so, there were many other ways people used the land. Some of these, like tin-mining, have a history almost as long and rich as that of farming. In this chapter, I will review a selection of the ones that have had the greatest impact on the character of the county's historic landscape.

Fig. 68. Flooding in the Culm valley, looking north-east from Paddleford Bridge.
Frances Griffith/DCC, SX99 23rd February1994.

WATERMEADOWS

Meadows have always been important in Devon's agricultural economy, particularly those lying along the bottom of river valleys. Meadows occurred in other places too, but as discussed in Chapter 3 it can be hard to distinguish them from arable land without detailed documentary or archaeological research. This is because fields could be used for different purposes over time: a field once used for arable might later have been used as pasture or meadow. The form of a field's boundaries may preserve evidence of only one episode in a long history.

We can be fairly certain that land on flat valley-bottoms and on the damp slopes close to streams was often managed as meadow in the past. The valley-bottoms were particularly prone to flooding, especially in winter, when enriching alluvium might be washed down and deposited over them (fig. 68). In many parts of England, such meadows were divided into strips like the arable land further up the hillside, but were assigned by lots when the hay

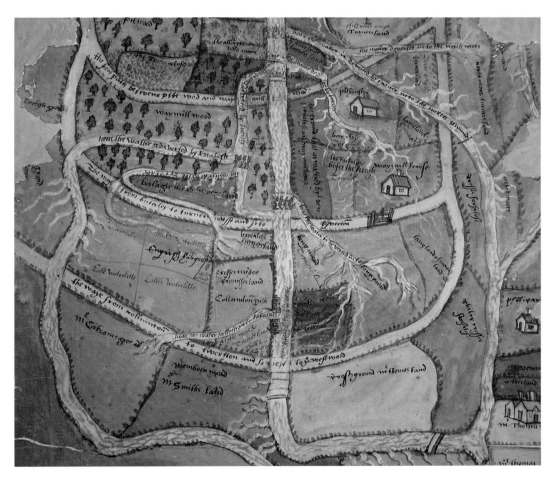

Fig. 69.   Manuscript map dating to 1603-8 showing land in Halberton, north-east Devon. The map was made to provide evidence in a dispute about rights over the water supply, and it vividly illustrates the importance attached to watering the hillside meadows at this date.
Reproduced by kind permission of Devon Record Office, DRO 6065Z/E1.

81

was ready to be cut (Brian 1999). Harold Fox's research on Axminster showed how valley-bottom meadow was sometimes divided into strips by the 13th century in Devon, with particular strips belonging to particular holdings (Fox 1972: 114).

The term 'watermeadow' has a specific meaning in central parts of Wessex. It refers to the elaborate systems of hatches, leats and channels which conducted water over the flat surface of the fields. Huge areas of watermeadow earthworks still exist in places like the Avon valley south of Salisbury and along the River Itchen close to Winchester. Such watermeadows probably originated in the 16th century, and became increasingly widespread and complicated in the 17th and 18th (Rackham 1986: 339; Bettey 1999). However, this is not the meaning implied by the term 'watermeadow' in the Devon HLC. Here it has been used to signify all types of meadow that were periodically inundated, whether by nature or design.

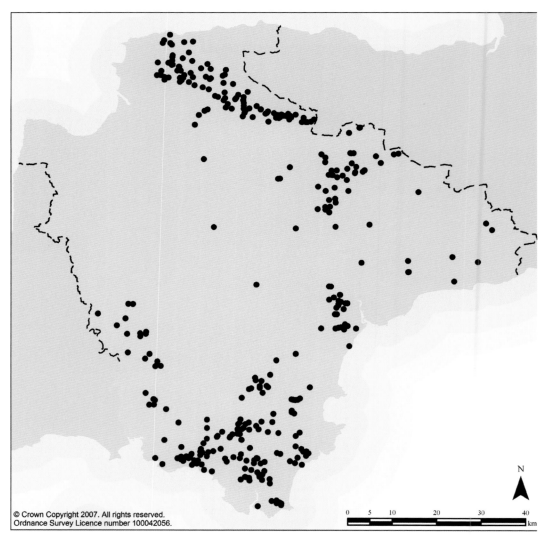

Fig. 70.   Distribution of probable post-medieval catchmeadows, *c.* 1890, based on the Devon HLC

The flow of water across the fields has a long history in Devon, even if it was done less formally than in the great post-medieval watermeadows of Wessex. The early Devon watermeadows had far less intricate systems of leats, but they still involved watering the fields to increase their fertility and encourage the early growth of grass. Sometimes, this was deliberately managed: in west Devon, for example, Harold Fox has discovered 15th century references to cleaning out channels in a meadow at Cargoll (Fox 1991b: 315-6). At other times, the flow of waters might not have been deliberately controlled, the meadows just being left to flood naturally (Griffith 1988: 119). For the purposes of the Devon HLC, much valley-bottom land has been mapped as 'probable watermeadow' where it lay as fields in the later 19th century. This is very likely to have been its normal use since at least the later Middle Ages.

There were two types of deliberately watered meadows in Devon from the late medieval period onwards. The first were the valley-bottom meadows. Some good examples of these are clearly depicted on a manuscript map of Haccombe in south Devon dating to around the turn of the 16th century (partly reproduced by Gray 2003: 122). The map shows how water was deliberately diverted from the little stream into the fields through leats and channels. Later on, similar but more elaborate and regular systems were created during the 18th and 19th century heyday of Wessex watermeadows, like those in the Exe valley to the south of Tiverton.

A second type of watermeadow has left even more distinctive traces across much of Devon's landscape. These are the hillside meadows known variously as 'catch meadows', 'catchwater' or 'catchwork meadows', or 'field-gutter' systems. They too have a very long

Fig. 71. The earthworks of catchmeadow systems show clearly on the hillsides around Walscott, North Molton. In several places on the photograph, the catchmeadow leats can be seen cutting through earlier boundaries between fields and strip divisions. Photo: © getmapping, 2000.

Fig. 72.   The only leat of the catchmeadow system still in use at Walscott.
Photo: Sam Turner, October 2003.

history in Devon, and it seems likely they were already common by the end of the 16th century. For example, an early catchwork system seems to be shown on a manuscript map dating to shortly after 1600 that shows the land around Moorstone Barton in Halberton, north-east Devon. It clearly depicts an intricate system of leats on the gentle slopes around the settlements (fig. 69). By the end of the 18th century the practice was widespread, and the agricultural writer William Marshall believed that west Devon's watermeadows were second only to those of central Wessex in terms of their productivity (Marshall 1796a: 207-9). The aim of catchmeadows was not to irrigate the land, but to use water to raise the average temperature of the ground in early spring so that the grass would start growing earlier. In theory, this meant the farmer would be able to get stock out into the fields earlier than his competitors. Whether it worked or not is uncertain, but in certain parts of Devon and neighbouring counties they became very popular.

Catchmeadows take the form of parallel leats or 'gutters' that follow the contour of the hillside. Often, the water was channelled through a farmyard first so that it could have manure mixed in with it (which also helped clean out the yard) (Riley & Wilson-North 2001: 128-9). The leats normally seem to have been fairly shallow – perhaps 50cm or so in depth – though most have now silted up and survive only as slight earthworks on the hillsides.

Very few Devon catchmeadows are still in use. I have seen one on the southern fringes of Exmoor at Walscott Farm, North Molton (figs 71 & 72). Here the farmer still uses one gutter to water the hillside below the deserted farmstead at Lower Walscott in the spring. He remembers that when he was a boy, much more of the system was in operation. It seems he was never particularly convinced of its efficacy, so most of it has since fallen into disrepair. At one time, though, people must have thought catchmeadows were worth the significant investment required to create them: extensive earthworks in many parts of Devon still show where they were built. In the South Hams, the central part of the Exe valley around Tiverton, and along the southern side of Exmoor, catchmeadows were particularly common. Even now, they are a highly distinctive aspect of the rural landscape in these areas (fig. 70).

It is hard to say how many valley-bottom fields are still permanently used as traditional meadowland. In the south and east, improvements in drainage during the 20th century and the decline in demand for hay mean that much of this fertile land is now used for arable crops. In other places, particularly the north-west, much that might once have been meadow has become overgrown with scrubby woodland. Of around 100km² mapped for *c*.1890 in the Devon HLC, only about a quarter has seen relatively little change during the 20th century.

ORCHARDS

Orchards are strongly associated with Devon, particularly apple trees for cider production. They have a long history: in 14th and 15th century Plymstock tenants of Tavistock Abbey

Fig. 73.   Filling sacks with apples, West Park Farm, Iddesleigh, Devon, 1986.
Photograph by James Ravilious (copyright James Ravilious).

Fig. 74.   In the field beyond the polytunnels, the regular earthworks of a former
orchard are visible at Holcombe, Ottery St Mary. The depressions in the fields
to either side are marl pits. Photo: Sam Turner, November 2005.

were using the abbot's cider press and shipping some of their produce back along the Tamar
to the monks (Finberg 1951: 196).

In most of Devon, virtually every farmstead and hamlet once had its own orchards (Fig.
73). In some regions these could be quite extensive. The HLC shows that in the 1890s there
were around 120km^2 of orchards in Devon, equivalent to about 29,700 acres – far more
than previously estimated (see e.g. Overton 2006: 125). Because the HLC concentrated
on mapping different character types in blocks greater than 1 hectare, this figure will not
include many small orchards, so the true total must have been greater still. It is also clear
from the HLC that not all parts of Devon had the same number of fruit trees. They are

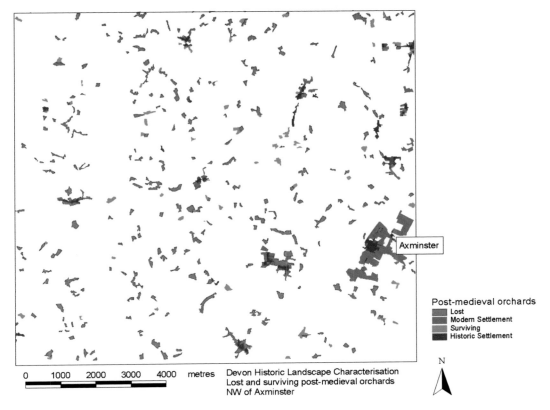

Post-medieval orchards
Lost
Modern Settlement
Surviving
Historic Settlement

0   1000   2000   3000   4000   metres   Devon Historic Landscape Characterisation
Lost and surviving post-medieval orchards
NW of Axminster

Axminster

N

Fig. 75.   The loss of historic orchards since the 1890s in the area around Axminster, east Devon.

completely absent from the high moors of course, but they are also thin on the ground in other places: in north-west Devon, for example, there were often tiny orchards close to the farmhouse, but they were very rarely as big as those found elsewhere. If anything, this probably reflects environmental factors: apple trees do not like overly wet conditions, and late frosts will severely affect the apple crop. The high ground of the North West and the moors are the parts of Devon most exposed to the wind, rain and weather.

The image of a farmstead with tightly-clustered buildings set amongst apple orchards is highly evocative of the Devon countryside. Despite epitomising the county's ordinary rural landscapes, the number of orchards in Devon declined sharply in the 20th century. But even when they have gone, orchards leave distinctive traces in the landscape. Besides the evidence of Ordnance Survey maps, we can often detect where orchards used to be from the earthwork ridges that were originally made to keep the roots of newly-planted apple trees dry (fig. 74). The HLC shows clearly that the number of orchards in Devon has declined incredibly steeply in the last 100 years or so. Today, there are only around 4,700 acres remaining – an astonishing loss of 25,000 acres (100km^2) of fruit trees *at the very least* (fig. 75). In many places, this reduction has completely transformed the look and feel of the landscape: at Coombe in Ottery St Mary, for example, there is now only one small orchard where there were once 22 (fig. 76). Over the last fifteen years, however, organisations like Common Ground have campaigned for the value of orchards to be recognised (Common Ground 2000). New agri-environment schemes like Higher Level Stewardship are rewarding

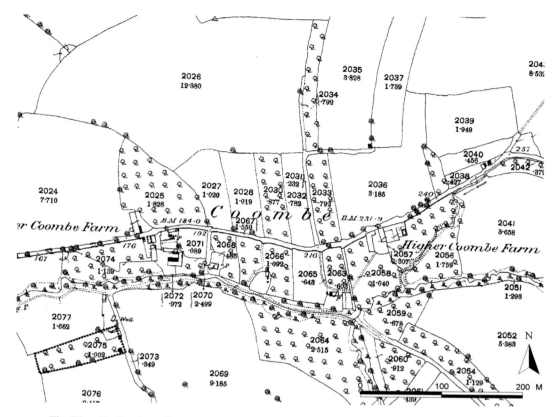

Fig. 76. Orchards at Coombe, Ottery St Mary, 1889. The dotted line shows the only one of these orchards to survive to the present. 1st edn OS 1:2,500 map, 1889. Map reproduced by kind permission of Landmark. © and database right Crown copyright and Landmark Information Group Ltd (all rights reserved 2007).

landowners for managing and restoring their orchards (see Chapter 6), and recently there has been a small rise in the area of Devon orchards.

PARKS AND LARGE GARDENS

Around more important houses, orchards were often planted as elements in extensive gardens and parks. These have been mapped in the Devon HLC as a separate category, although a rather wide ranging one: it includes not only private parks and substantial gardens, but also allotments, public parks, and ornamental landscaping of all sorts. The term 'designed landscape' is often used to describe such areas, though for the purposes of the HLC we felt this was too imprecise – after all, most of the landscape types mapped for our project were 'designed' in one way or another.

Ornamental parks and gardens have existed in Devon since the Middle Ages (Iles 1994). There were as many as 60 deer parks in the county which provided the landed elite with venues for leisure and sport. Often these parks lay around a great house – the deer park at Okehampton Castle on the northern fringes of Dartmoor provides a good example – but sometimes they were separate, standing isolated in the farming landscape. Most of Devon's medieval deerparks were 'disparked' in the early modern period, so the only indicators of their former existence are usually traces of park pales, the deerpark boundaries built of earth and stone, and occasionally other features such as lodges or platforms for watching the hunt (Iles 1994). When they were disparked they were normally turned to some agricultural use. At Crediton Great Park, for example, the Bishop of Exeter's former deerpark was converted into several smallish holdings when it was acquired by the Dennis family in the 16th century, each with neatly bounded fields and farmstead. Several centuries of farming normally mean the contribution of medieval deerparks to the character of Devon's landscape today is only very slight.

A more lasting legacy has resulted from the construction of formal gardens around many houses between the 15th and 17th centuries. These include not only major late medieval and Tudor houses like Dartington (Currie 2003) or Holcombe Rogus (Griffith 1988: Pl. 72), but also the smaller 'barton'-type farmhouses of the local gentry. Many such houses had small formal gardens, with water features, terraces, and ornamental planting. Though they have often been altered by subsequent redesigns, traces of them remain around houses like Keynedon Barton and Painsford in the South Hams (Waterhouse 2003). At Holcombe Burnell Barton, terraced gardens were created by the Dennis family in the 16th century within what had formerly been a medieval deerpark. They seem to have enclosed much of the remainder for farming, as they had also done in the deerpark at Crediton.

Fashions in garden design changed several times in the post-medieval period. In the 18th century many old terraced gardens were altered in pursuit of more open landscapes, and many acres of fields were incorporated into extensive parks. It is often these that

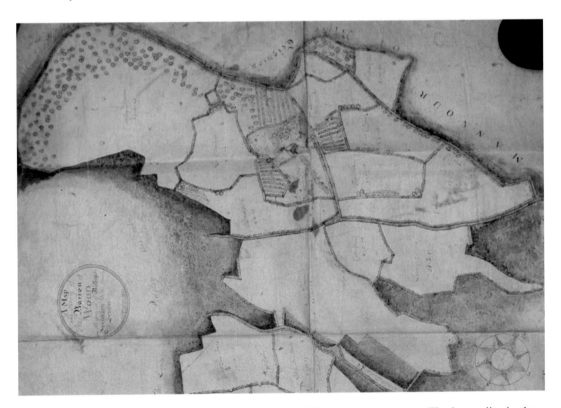

Fig. 77.   Wood, Bishopsteignton, as depicted on an 18th-century estate map. The house lies in the centre, surrounded by orchards. DRO 1039M-E61, reproduced by kind permission of Mr B. Comyns.

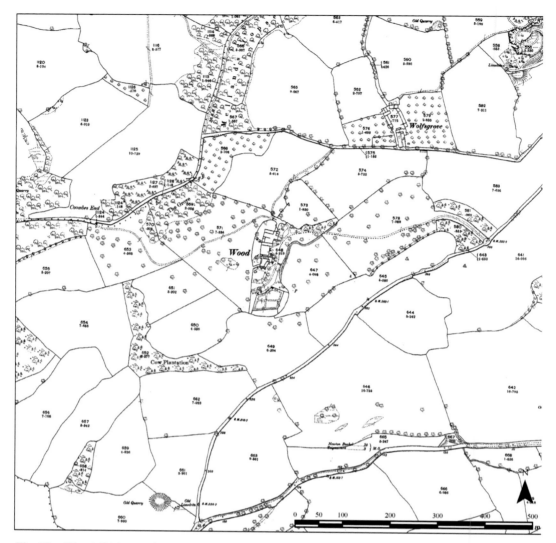

Fig. 78. Wood, Bishopsteignton, as depicted on the 1st edn OS 1:2,500 map, 1889. The fields around the house have been reorganised; orchards have been removed and other fields have been planted with trees to create a more extensive park. The drive to the house from the Bishopsteignton-Kingsteignton road has also been moved. Map reproduced by kind permission of Landmark. © and database right Crown copyright and Landmark Information Group Ltd (all rights reserved 2007).

have left the most distinctive traces in today's landscape. They include not only great examples created by important families, places like Castle Hill (Filleigh), Powderham and Knightshayes (fig. 77), but also very many smaller parks created around lesser houses following similar principles. There are many examples: Wood, near Bishopsteignton, shows the transformation to a parkland landscape in the 19th century (Figs 78 & 79).

For the Devon HLC these parks and gardens have been identified from the historic OS maps and modern aerial photographs, with additional information from English Heritage's *Register of Parks and Gardens*. The whole park has been mapped as a single character type,

Fig. 79.   Knightshayes, Tiverton: a Victorian country house and garden.
Photo: Bill Horner/DCC, 7th June 1994.

even when it contained significant blocks of woodland or stretches of water. Unquestionably, this is not a complete database: the surviving traces of many parks and gardens are either too small or not sufficiently distinct to have been mapped.

Nevertheless, the HLC mapping reveals some interesting information about parks and gardens in Devon. It is little surprise to learn that their nature and extent has changed greatly since the 1890s. Many country houses have wholly or partly disappeared, as at Stevenstone (St Giles in the Wood), Fowelscombe (Ugborough) and Haldon House (Kenn) (Gray 2003: 122), and virtually all parks have seen at least some land turned over to more intensive agricultural use in the 20th century. Many parks on the edges of towns are now used for purposes other than those first intended: thus Streatham Hall now accommodates the University of Exeter, and Follaton House (Totnes) is the headquarters for South Hams District Council. Some parkland survives at both, but inevitably new offices, car parks and access roads change the feel of such places. The HLC also shows whereabouts in the county most of these parks have been built. Whilst parks were established in more or less all areas in the 19th century, there were particular clusters around major towns like Plymouth,

Fig. 80. Mixed woodland in the Tamar valley (SX382729). The partially
stone-faced bank on the right-hand side forms the outer boundary
of an historic field system. Photo: Sam Turner, July 2006.

Torquay and Barnstaple. The greatest concentration was in the countryside around the
county town of Exeter: 35% of all Devon parkland was less than 20km (12½ miles) from
the city centre in 1890. Today, around 30% of parks and gardens are found in the same area;
the slight difference is mainly due to the fact the HLC of the modern landscape includes
numerous public parks in urban areas like Plymouth and Torbay.

WOODLAND

The presence of trees and woodland makes a crucial contribution to the character of any landscape. In Devon today there is at least 620km^2 of woodland, enough to cover virtually the whole of Exmoor National Park in a continuous canopy of trees. The management of trees by people has shaped the landscape here since earliest times. The wildwood that grew up after the last glaciation was cut and burnt by people from at least the Mesolithic period (c.5000 BC) onwards, and substantial clearances accompanied the rise of agriculture during the Neolithic. Because trees have always been used and managed by people, they are not only 'natural', but also a fundamental part of our historic landscape (Clare & Bunce 2006; Barnes & Williamson 2006). Up until the mid-19th century, woodland was economically very important, providing resources for a range of purposes. In the Middle Ages, for example, woodland provided not only building materials and fuel, but also grazing ground for pigs and other animals (Cannell 2005: 149-55). Woods in the lowlands and round the fringes of the moors were probably particularly heavily exploited, and archaeological evidence in the form of charcoal burning platforms and water channels reveals how their importance to rural industry intensified during the historic periods (Gerrard 1997: 94; Cannell 2005: 186-90).

Woodland occurs in almost all parts of Devon, although the distribution varies. In some parishes, like Newton St Cyres north-east of Dartmoor and Wembworthy in central Devon, nearly 20% of the land is covered with trees. Elsewhere woodland is much more sparsely scattered, with less than 1% of Bradworthy or Newton St Petrock in north-west Devon being wooded, and no woods at all in the wind-blasted valleys of South Huish. Old woodland is mainly located on the steep valley sides. The largest contiguous patches are found in major river valleys like those of the Taw, Torridge and Tamar (fig. 80), and the steep coombes that fringe Dartmoor and Exmoor. The Devon HLC has mapped three main types of woodland, and I will briefly discuss each in turn. These are 'ancient woodland', 'other woodland' and 'conifer plantations'.

Ancient Woodland
There are various definitions of 'ancient woodland', but most writers use the term for woods that have existed for a minimum of 300-400 years (Rackham 2003; Kirby & Goldberg 2002-3). Because many have been subject to continuous management, ancient *woods* will not necessarily include ancient *trees*, though they often do. An ancient wood might also contain many different types of *woodland* (e.g. different combinations of species), perhaps because various species prefer particular soil types or because certain areas have been managed in different ways (Rackham 1986: 103). The Devon HLC largely followed English Nature's definition, which identifies a wood as 'ancient' if it has existed continuously in the same place since about 1600 (Kirby & Goldberg 2002-3). However, unlike English Nature's *Inventory of Ancient Woodland*, the HLC mapping does not include plantations on ancient woodland sites in this category. Such plantations often cause significant disruption to both plant communities and archaeological features, and the HLC has generally mapped them as 'other woodland' or 'conifers' (see below).

English Nature's provisional *Inventory* was used as an additional source to help identify which woods ought to be included in this category for the HLC. This was the GIS version available in 2001, although it has since been updated (English Nature 2006; note that English Nature became part of a new organisation called 'Natural England' in October 2006). Because of the scale at which it operates, the Devon HLC was able to suggest a few improvements on the original version of the *Inventory*. Firstly, the English Nature dataset only includes woodlands bigger than 2 hectares: the HLC added some smaller woods. Secondly, it was possible to suggest a few corrections to the *Inventory* based on the sources available to the HLC, including recent air photography and the digital 1st edition OS maps.

Nevertheless, the mapping for the HLC was deliberately very conservative, and only woods thought very likely indeed to represent ancient woodland were included. It is very hard to distinguish the tree species in a wood or the size of trees from maps and air photographs, and virtually impossible to detect features like old coppice and pollards. The best way to get a really sound idea of the composition of a wood is surely to visit it (Cannell 2005). As a result it is very likely that many areas of woodland mapped as 'other woodland' in the HLC should really have been put in the 'ancient woodland' category.

Historical, archaeological and scientific research all combine to suggest that Devon's ancient woodlands really are very old indeed. Oliver Rackham's analysis of Domesday Book entries suggested that around 4% of the county was wooded in 1086, much of it in small woods of under 17 acres (Rackham 1986: 78). Going back further, palaeoenvironmental research in mid- and north Devon suggests much of the woodland cover at lower and middle altitudes was well established by the early Middle Ages (Fyfe *et al.* 2003; Fyfe 2006). Nearby, detailed work by Judith Cannell in the valleys around Exmoor has shown that the boundaries of many ancient woodlands were relatively stable during the Middle Ages (Cannell 2005: 189). Occasionally, distinctive wavy edges betray the sites of late-medieval or early modern assarting (clearance for farming) that has eaten into earlier woodlands (e.g. in Axminster: Fox 1972, fig. 47). In Devon, however, this seems to be the exception rather than the rule, and we must be wary of identifying it based only on the shape of woodlands. Similar wavy edges might be created for a number of reasons. For example, by examining 19th century maps of Dawlish we can see that the wavy field boundaries bordering woodland on the north side of Aller Farm were created in the 19th century when the woodland of Luscombe Park was extended down the hillside (Finneran & Turner 2003).

Fig. 81.   Scrubby woodland advancing from the valley of the River Plym on the remains of a prehistoric settlement preserved in moorland at Dewerstone, Meavy.
Photo: Frances Griffith/DCC, Dewerstone SX5363, 12th May 1989.

Other Woodland

Other mixed and broadleaved woods have been mapped as 'other woodland'. As noted above, this category probably includes quite large areas of Devon's 'ancient' woodland, because it is hard to identify securely without making field visits. However, it also contains much more recent woods. During the later 19th and 20th centuries, there has been a significant encroachment of scrubby woodland around the edges of moorland and in neglected fields and valley bottoms (fig. 81). It is not uncommon to find old hedgebanks within such woodland, showing where trees have grown up on land once managed as fields of one sort or another. Rather counter-intuitively, it is clear from the HLC that there are far more trees in Devon today than there were 100 years ago. Even discounting conifer plantations (see below), the growth in woodland is striking. In the 1890s, there were around 371km² of ancient, broadleaved and mixed woodland. Today that figure is at least 506km² – an increase of over 36%. Given that the recent growth of woodland was well underway by the end of the 19th century, we can be fairly certain that Devon is more wooded now than at any other time in the last millennium.

Conifer Plantations

The final type of tree-cover mapped for the HLC is conifer plantations. Some historical ecologists have very strong feelings about conifer plantations, which they believe do not merit the title of 'woodland' (see for example Rackham 1986: 153). Even so, they are included as a separate category in the HLC since there are significant areas in Devon that have long provided distinctive elements of the rural landscape (fig. 82). Conifers were first planted on any scale in the 18th century. Between then and about 1950 their numbers increased exponentially. Many were planted as landscape features in parks and gardens, and some were used as shelter belts for exposed farmland (as at Cator on Dartmoor). Most formed extensive plantations. So, for example, in the late 18th century, Francis Buller tried to plant 40,000 trees on his estate at Prince Hall near Two Bridges on Dartmoor (Somers Cocks 1970: 268). His attempts were apparently unsuccessful, but elsewhere entrepreneurs had more luck: the large-scale conifer plantation established on Ausewell Common near Ashburton in the mid-19th century still dominates the skyline from miles around. Plantations were not only made on Dartmoor, and by the end of the 19th century there were larches and pines growing on former rough ground from Uplyme in the east to Gulworthy in the west, and in north Devon parishes like Buckland Filleigh, Petrockstow and East Worlington. By 1900 at least 44km² of conifers had been planted in the county. However, it was the first half of the 20th century that saw the greatest number of trees planted. After the Forestry Commission was established in 1919 the area under plantations was more than doubled in response to the perceived need for more home-grown timber. Great swathes of Dartmoor were dedicated to larches and firs in the 1920s, 30s and 40s at places like Fernworthy, Bellever and Soussons Down (Somers Cocks 1970: 267-71). Away from Dartmoor, huge plantations were also established on the Haldon Ridge near Exeter (at least 13.5km²) and at Cookworthy Moor in the parishes of Ashwater, Black Torrington and Halwill (*c.*7km²). In many of Devon's steep river valleys, ancient broadleaved woodland was cut down and replaced with commercial conifer plantations. For example, along a 6.5km-stretch of the River Tavy between Anderton and Marystow in west Devon, some 246 hectares (608 acres) of plantations now grow where there were once native hardwoods.

All told, there are today around 108km² of conifer plantations in the area studied for the Devon HLC, bringing the total area under woodland of one sort or another to at least 614km² (*c.* 151,700 acres). This is about 9.5% of the total study area. It represents a remarkable increase in the number of Devon woods: if Rackham's estimate from Domesday Book is correct (Rackham 1986: 78), there is around twice as much woodland growing in the county today as there was 1,000 years ago.

Fig. 82.   A Tamar valley conifer plantation. Photo: Sam Turner, July 2006.

THE ROUGH GROUND

Beyond the fields and woods lies Devon's rough ground. There are many different kinds. Above all the great grim expanse of Dartmoor sits like a giant boss of granite, dominating views for miles in all directions. Smaller patches of heath and moory ridges are still common in many corners of the county, though much diminished now compared to their former extents. Along the bottoms of small valleys, stands of gorse and bracken give way to marshy vegetation following little streams. By the sea, wild cliff-tops and expanses of dunes once provided important grazing grounds. With the exception of marshes (salt and freshwater), dunes, mud and sand, all these landscapes have been included in the 'rough ground' category for the Devon HLC. Nevertheless, local research will show that blocks of rough ground in different places have widely varying plant communities depending on the local geology, environment and historic management practices.

The nature and potential of the soil has clearly affected how it was used in the past. Rough grazing ground occupies much less land in the South Hams than in north-west Devon: the brown soils of the former are more easily worked and more fertile than the Culm Measures of north Devon and Cornwall. Even so, rough grazing land still occupied an important place in the South Hams' landscape and historic agricultural system: stock were grazed on the sea cliffs or taken up to Dartmoor for the summer months (Fox 1994; 2005; forthcoming). The Moor, which was visible from hilltops throughout the district, also played a central part in local folklore (Franklin 2006). Furthermore, just because ground is not intensively farmed today or is hard to work, we must assume neither that it had no value

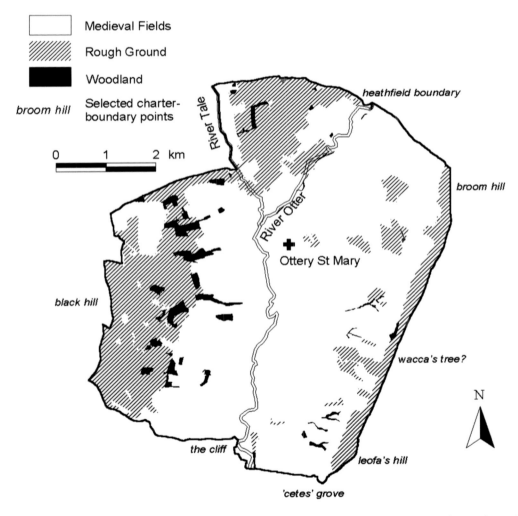

Fig. 83.   Ottery St Mary (Devon) and selected boundary points from a late-Saxon charter boundary clause (S1033; after Hooke 1994). HLC data from Devon HLC (Turner 2006a, fig. 46).

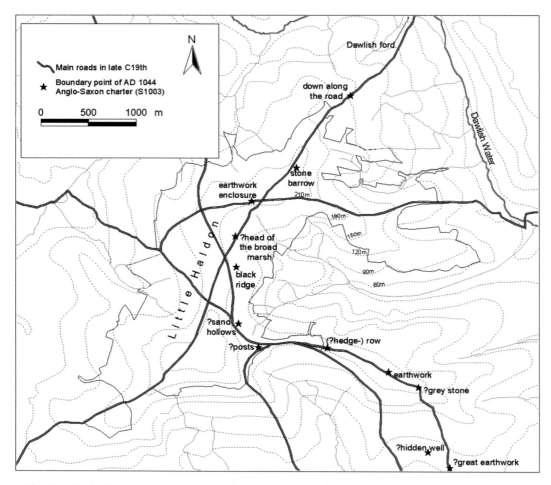

Fig. 84. Part of the late-Saxon charter boundary of Dawlish (S1003, see Hooke 1994). The 1820s estate boundary mapped in fig. 49 follows part of the same boundary; the estate map shows the section from the 'earthwork enclosure' (Castle Dyke) and past the barrow on along the road (Finneran & Turner 2003, fig. 5).

to earlier farmers, nor that it could not be worked with sufficient effort. Chris Caseldine has argued that virtually none of the soils of south-west England are too poor to support human populations, especially considering the relatively minor climatic fluctuations of the last 5,000 years (Caseldine 1999); the abundant evidence for cultivation on hills and moorlands throughout Devon in prehistoric and historic periods proves that people used much of this land for arable in earlier times (see below).

Environmental studies suggest that there were areas naturally free from tree cover on Dartmoor even before people began regularly to make clearings for agriculture. Increasing levels of clearance by people in the late Mesolithic and Neolithic led both to agricultural activity on the moors and the natural growth of blanket peat. Intensive farming on the moors seems to have reached its greatest extent during the Bronze Age, when huge areas were enclosed in stone-walled fields (their remains are discussed further below; Gerrard 1997). From the Iron Age onwards, Dartmoor was less intensively occupied – very few sites have been identified on the moors that date to the last millennium BC or the first millennium AD. Nevertheless, Dartmoor and other moorlands were almost certainly still used for pasture and other resources (Rackham 1986: 309).

Other, smaller areas of rough ground probably have similar histories. For example, archaeological evidence proves the heathy hilltops of the Haldon Ridge were settled in the Neolithic (Gent & Quinnell 1999). Ralph Fyfe's palaeoenvironmental research in mid-Devon shows that the amount of heathy ground at lower altitudes may have increased and stabilised after *c.* AD 800, suggesting it was a useful part of the agricultural system there (Fyfe 2006). Where documentary records cast any light on this issue, it seems that areas of rough ground lay at the margins of many estates and in some valley bottoms during the early Middle Ages. An eleventh-century Anglo-Saxon charter boundary clause for Ottery St Mary in east Devon mentions several landmarks typical of the rough ground, for example the 'heathfield boundary', 'broom hill' and 'black hill' (fig. 83; Hooke 1994). On Little Haldon above Dawlish, another boundary-clause describes how the estate ran up along a 'Black Ridge', round the 'head of a broad marsh' before using several prehistoric monuments as marker points, including a hillfort and two barrows (Finneran & Turner 2003). Interestingly, the same archaeological sites still acted as boundary markers in the early 19th century, when the area in question was still unenclosed heathland (figs 84 & 49).

A slightly later charter from the same area uses a *ferngara*, or 'ferny gore', as a boundary line (Hooke 1994: 213-6). A 'gore' is a narrow valley, and it seems this one was rough ground in the 11th century. All over Devon and Cornwall there have always been areas of rough grazing at lower altitudes than the hilltops, moors and ridges, whether long narrow strips on valley-bottoms not used as meadow (common in north-west Devon), or largely open areas like the Downs in Cardinham and Warleggan south-west of Bodmin Moor (Turner 2006a). In historic agricultural systems, the rough ground had a diverse range of uses, including not only summer grazing and occasional outfield arable, but also quarrying, bee-keeping, and the cutting of peat ('turf') for fuel, gorse ('furze') for animal fodder and bracken ('ferns') for bedding, thatching and ropemaking (Herring 2004).

Fig. 85 . The view north-east across Woodland Wood to Dartmoor from near Cudlipptown, Peter Tavy. Much of the scrubby woodland in the valley of the Tavy here has grown up in the 20th century. Photo: Sam Turner, July 2006.

In the late 19th and 20th centuries, most of these traditional uses for the rough ground ceased to be useful for Devon's farmers. As a National Park, the great expanse of Dartmoor has retained its grazing animals, and has also gained a new importance for its amenity, recreation and conservation potential. Where smaller areas of rough ground survived into the 20th century their fortunes have been more varied. Much has been enclosed and drained as farmland; elsewhere, especially in the valley bottoms, small patches of rough ground are no longer useful for modern farmers: many are now overgrown with thorns and scrubby woodland (fig. 85).

Nevertheless, the history of the rough ground is far from simple (Hoskins 1954). It has not just shrunk and shrunk from a hypothetical maximum in the Mesolithic or Neolithic, but instead shows a complex history of encroachment and recovery from episodes of settled agriculture, woodland and industry. The archaeological evidence preserved in the historic landscape provides eloquent testimony to several of these phases.

Prehistoric Fields in the Rough Ground

Devon is unusual in England and Europe because the rough ground of its uplands preserves extensive tracts of prehistoric fields. Dartmoor in particular has become justly famous for its Bronze Age landscapes, which include not only settlements and burial sites but also the fields that went with them (Fleming 1988; 1994a; Gerrard 1997). Their outlines have been mapped for the HLC using air photos and the results of English Heritage's extensive field survey programme. The largest areas are to be found on the eastern side of the moor, but there are smaller areas in many places round its fringes.

The remains of two main types of prehistoric field systems are found on the Moor. The first, and the most famous, have become generally known by their local name, 'reaves'. They

Fig. 86.   Parallel reaves on Corndon Down, Dartmoor.
Photo: Frances Griffith/DCC, SX67NE230, 13th September 1994.

Fig. 87.   Medieval and modern fields on the edge of Chagford Common on the eastern side of Dartmoor appear to share the same alignment as their prehistoric predecessors, hinting that medieval farmers re-used existing prehistoric boundaries (shown in yellow, based on the results of an RCHM(E)/EH 1:10,000 field survey). Photo: © getmapping, 2000.

consist of long parallel boundary banks that march across the landscape for miles, often ignoring intervening topographical features like river valleys or rocky tors. Subdivisions in the fields are marked by shorter banks between parallel reaves. The latter eventually end at so-called 'terminal reaves' running at right-angles (fig. 86). Archaeologists call the second category of prehistoric fields on the moors 'aggregated' fields, a term that refers to the way new enclosures were added to old ones such that we can often work out the sequence in which they were built. These fields are always associated with settlements, and hut circles nestle amongst them. Reaves and aggregated field systems seem to have been in use at the same time. In some places, reaves were attached to aggregated fields, but elsewhere it was the other way round (Gerrard 1997: 53-4).

Many of these ancient fields now lie amidst Dartmoor's heather and bracken. In places we can see how medieval and later farmers used the reaves as the basis of their own field systems: the historic boundaries of medieval and modern fields continue on the same alignment as the prehistoric ones lying today on open moorland, particularly around the southern and eastern fringes of Dartmoor (fig. 87) (Fleming & Ralph 1982; see e.g. Corndon

Fig. 88. Boundaries of a prehistoric field system preserved
in coastal rough ground at Deckler's Cliff, East Portlemouth.
Photo: Frances Griffith/DCC, SX73NE21 Deckler's Cliff, 29th July 1992.

Tor, Dartmoor: Gerrard 1997, fig. 76; Griffith 1988: 34). Occasionally prehistoric field systems have also been preserved in the Devon lowlands and around the coasts, particularly where they lay for centuries under coastal rough grazing: there are good examples on the clifftops near Beer and at East Portlemouth in the South Hams (fig. 88) (Griffith 1988: 45, 23; Newman 2003).

Abandoned Medieval and Post-Medieval Fields
As far as we can tell from the archaeological evidence, most of Dartmoor and the other high moors and heaths lay uncultivated in the Iron Age, Romano-British period and early Middle Ages (*c.*800 BC - AD 1000). Historical and place-name evidence suggests its main agricultural use during this time was probably for summer pastures (Gerrard 1997; Fox 2005). However, over the last millennium various farming episodes have left distinct traces on the rough grazing ground.

In Chapter 3 I used some Dartmoor examples to help illustrate the nature of Devon's medieval fields. Many of the farms established on the Moor in the later Middle Ages are still occupied and farmed, as at Challacombe (just!). However, many others have been abandoned: their fields, farmhouses, yards and gardens have gone back to the rough ground from which they were cut seven or eight centuries ago. At least 130 deserted medieval settlements are known on Dartmoor (Gerrard 1997: 71). John Allan's careful research on pottery assemblages from excavations at deserted moorland farms has shown that most were established after the middle of the 13th century, and abandoned by the middle of the 15th (Allan 1994). Some of the best-known examples are the hamlets to the east of Hound Tor (Manaton). Two small settlements with ruined longhouses, farm buildings and yards lie surrounded by overgrown medieval fields. Strip lynchets show how these enclosures were once subdivided between the tenants at the hamlets; the highly irregular form of the fields might not suggest this arrangement otherwise (fig. 89 & 48). Elsewhere it is common to find extensive earthworks of medieval field systems in the rough ground where it borders still-used fields with medieval origins. Challacombe is a good instance (Pattison 1999), but there are many others. On the west side of Dartmoor several good examples can be found in the small valleys on the eastern side of Peter Tavy. In some cases, it seems the fields have only become overgrown in quite recent times: walls and boundary banks are still clearly visible south of Wapworthy and Longbitter, and the fields were marked on the first edition Ordnance Survey map. In other places, abandonment took place longer ago: ridge and furrow and other earthworks south of Godsworthy have long been a feature of the moorland rough ground (fig. 28).

The earthworks and tumbled walls of medieval fields are not only found on the high moors. All over Devon, smaller patches of rough ground show evidence for earlier agricultural uses. Some of the best examples are found on little patches of moorland in mid- and north Devon. South of Newland Cross in Witheridge, where the ground rises to just over 200m above OD, a single field of rough ground has survived modern ploughing. The remains of at least three medieval hedgebanks are preserved within it, together with a great deal of medieval or post-medieval ridge and furrow. On Witheridge Moor, less than 2km to the east, more medieval hedgebanks and cultivation ridges lie amongst the heather and

Fig. 89. A reconstruction of the medieval settlement at Houndtor as it may have been before its desertion. Illustration © Rosemary Robertson (from DNPA 2002).

Fig. 90.   Ruined remains of the deserted post-medieval settlement at Little Comfort.
Photo: Peter Weddell (Exeter Museums Archaeological Field Unit),
15th February 1983. Source: Devon HER.

bracken, preserved in the rough ground along with prehistoric barrows and standing stones. Hare's Down and Rackenford Moor in Knowstone and Rackenford provide an outstanding example of an area of rough ground with extensive earlier features. There are the remains of field banks and ditches, ridge and furrow, and several deserted settlements. Hare's Down also testifies to the way arable cultivation and enclosure periodically breaks into the rough ground: there are not only medieval remains here, but also farms dating to the 17th-19th centuries (fig. 90). The surveyed boundaries and little conifer plantations at Little Comfort and Middle Ground distinguish them from their medieval predecessors, even though their creators reused some of the earlier medieval hedgebanks. Little Comfort, first recorded in 1679 is now deserted too: its neglected fields, sliced through by the new North Devon Link Road, look as though they will return to rough ground before too long.

This fluctuation in the extent of the rough ground is not unusual in Devon. On the contrary, if we take the long view it seems entirely typical. The history of the rough ground over the last 250 years is not a simple story. The HLC shows clearly that there is much less rough ground today than there was 100 years ago: about 685km^2 now (including Dartmoor) as opposed to 1,157km^2 then. However, if we cross-reference the HLC with the early 19th century Tithe Maps, we can see that attempts had already been made to farm much of this land in the 18th or early 19th centuries. In some places, as at Hound Tor, this post-medieval agriculture took place within the bounds of the existing medieval fields, as shown by the earthworks of narrow post-medieval cultivation ridges; in the spring the bluebells only flower here in the undisturbed medieval fields.

Elsewhere, as we saw in Chapter 3, landowners had laid out new enclosures across great

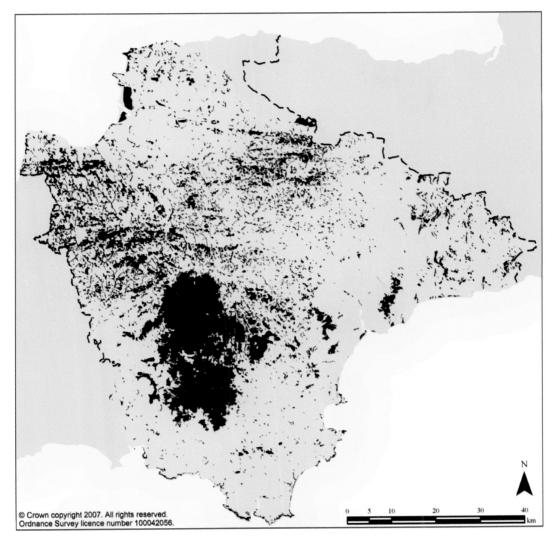

Fig. 91.   Rough ground in Devon, *c.* 1890. Source: Devon HLC.

swathes of rough ground in the century either side of 1800. On the 1st edition Ordnance Survey map, there are dead-straight boundaries dividing up areas of rough ground all over Devon: the result of agricultural improvements during the 18th and early 19th centuries. However, when the High Victorian farming boom ended in the 1870s, many of these fields went out of regular use and returned to rough grazing. Some have remained more or less uncultivated ever since. There are good examples on Dartmoor at places like Fox Tor and Crockern Tor, but others in lower-lying regions: on Broad Down (Farway) for example, and parts of Galsworthy Moors (Buckland Brewer). Having said this, the vast majority of this former rough ground off Dartmoor – some 330km^2 (around 81,500 acres) – is now firmly part of the modern farming landscape, and much of it is regularly under the plough.

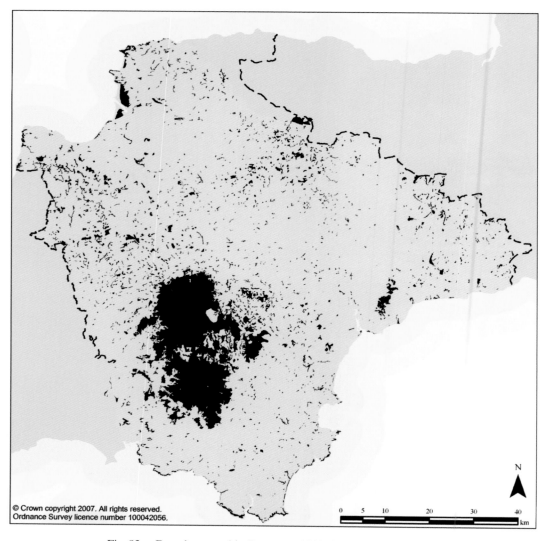

Fig. 92.   Rough ground in Devon, *c.* 2000. Source: Devon HLC.

MINING AND INDUSTRY

As we have seen in the last two chapters, the fields, woods and moors of rural Devon have been shaped by centuries of farming practice. Even so, farmers have never been the only people working in the countryside (or at least people have not always worked only at agriculture): many other endeavours have left distinctive traces on today's historic landscape. Some of the most widespread have been created by 'industries' of various kinds, especially quarrying, mining and related activities. The historic character of many areas has been deeply affected by medieval and later extractive industries.

The scale of the medieval metal industries is most obvious on Dartmoor, where extensive tin workings are found in many areas. Although various workings must have existed

106

in earlier times, it is from the Middle Ages onwards that this activity has left the most profound impact on today's historic landscapes (Thorndycraft *et al.* 2004). On Dartmoor and in the surrounding valleys, tin-bearing deposits have been worked on a large scale since at least the twelfth century (Newman 2006). For several hundred years, this activity was mostly limited to surface workings. Water from streams or artificial leats was used to separate tin ore (cassiterite) from the waste material or 'gangue' with which it was naturally deposited. These areas of 'streamworking' shaped huge swathes of moorland. The distinctive earthworks left behind include parallel banks of waste material and steep cuttings at the edges of the workings (Fig. 93). When the deposits nearest the surface were exhausted, the tinworkers began to dig downwards in search of their quarry. First they dug the cassiterite from pits, but when these could not be made deep enough they created 'openworks', deep, elongated cuttings reaching down to the tin ore deposits. Eventually, the tinners resorted to sinking shallow mines. Although it is not certain when mining for tin began, there had been medieval silver mines in Devon since the end of the 13th century, so it could have been quite early. The buildings, working areas, leats and reservoirs associated with tin working profoundly affected the moorland landscape (Gerrard 2000). The grassed-over remnants of medieval mining still scar the bottom of many moorland valleys. Mining-related remains have a massive historic significance for Devon and mining affected very large areas of the county. For these reasons, mining-related remains were mapped as a separate character

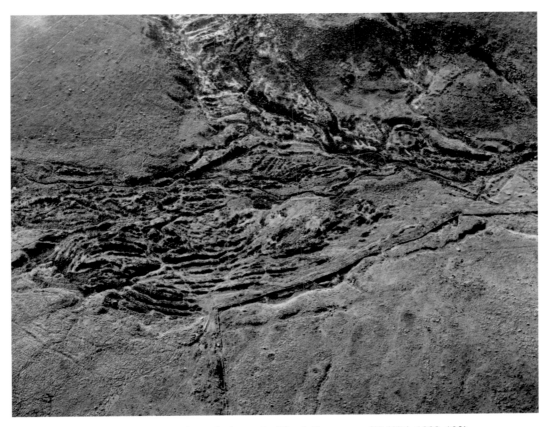

Fig. 93. Streamworks at Swincombe Head, Dartmoor (Griffith 1988: 102).
Photo: Frances Griffith/DCC 21st January 1988.

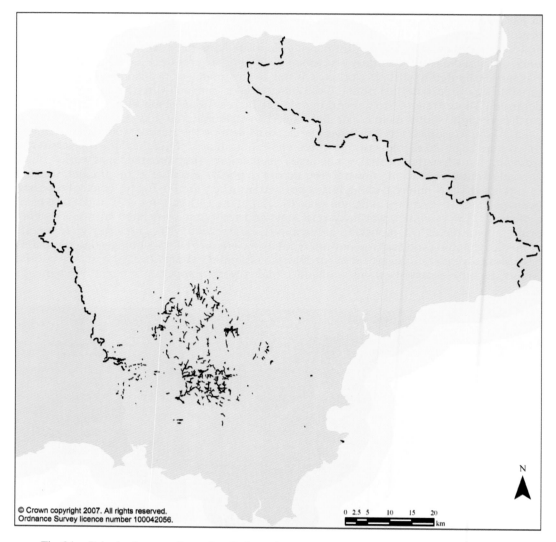

0 2.5 5   10   15   20
km

N

Fig. 94.   Principal areas of remains (influencing historic landscape character) from surface
workings or mining associated with metal working. Source: Devon HLC.

type in the Devon HLC. The results suggest the historic character of at least 14km² of
Dartmoor is dominated by medieval tin working remains: the results of a colossal human
earth-moving effort (fig. 94). Because mining remains often tend to stretch out for hundreds
of metres along the valley bottoms, the influence they exert on the overall character of the
landscape is quite disproportionate to their size.

In the 18th and 19th centuries, improved mining technology allowed deeper tin deposits
on Dartmoor to be worked through shaft mining (Gerrard 1997). These mines left
distinctively different remains to those of the medieval tinners. Not only was the cassiterite
extracted underground, but the mines were also serviced by different types of buildings.
They had distinctive areas for processing the ore, and created great spoil heaps of waste

Fig. 95.   Birchtor and Vitifer Mine showing streamworks, openworks, leats, trial pits and buildings (Griffith 1988: 102-3). Photo: Frances Griffith/DCC 21st January 1988.

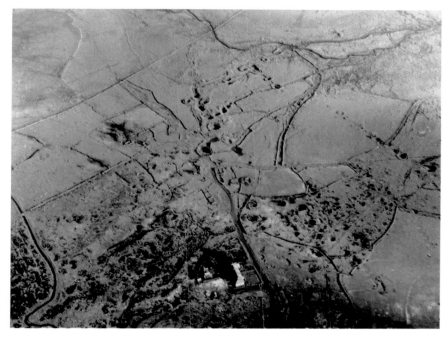

Fig. 96.   Whiteworks Mine, Hexworthy, Dartmoor (Griffith 1988: 103).
Photo: Frances Griffith/DCC 21st January 1988.

material (figs 95 & 96). Tin extraction was not the only industrial activity undertaken on Dartmoor, and other minerals and metals were also mined on the moor. Copper was particularly important, but other products included lead, arsenic, cobalt, silver, tungsten, zinc, and wolfram. Significant iron extraction took place around the fringes of the moor in mines at Haytor, South Brent and Ausewell Woods near Ashburton. Fuel to fire these industries came not only from wood charcoal, produced by the charcoal burners whose hearths lie scattered through the ancient woodlands, but also from peat charcoal: peat cutting has left significant earthworks across much of the Moor.

Quarries for granite and china clay became major industries in the mid-19th century. At Merrivale and Haytor there are major stone quarries with associated structures including industrial housing and tramways. The china clay industry, active up to the present, has affected a huge area of south-west Dartmoor: over 8km² has been totally transformed by the excavation of immense pits, spoil heaps and associated working areas (Booker 1970) (fig. 97).

Of course, mining and mineral extraction were not limited to Dartmoor. Around the fringes of Exmoor, for example, iron working took place from Roman times onwards; recent excavations have shown that there was an iron industry in the Blackdown Hills during the Roman, Anglo-Saxon and medieval periods (Reed *et al.* 2006). The low-lying heaths of the Teign and Bovey valleys between Dartmoor and the sea are pocked with pits and undulations providing evidence for past industries. There were sand-pits here, and tin-working by men who exploited alluvial deposits washed down from the moors. More significant in recent centuries have been the clay-pits, which originally provided the Bovey potteries with raw materials; great swathes of the valley floor between Kingsteignton and Chudleigh Knighton were consigned to this industry during the 20th century, and yawning

Fig. 97.   Crownhill Down, south-west Dartmoor, looking north. The great white scars are
china clay quarries. Photo: Frances Griffith/DCC, SX5659 25th July 1985.

Fig. 98   The ruined church of Holy Trinity, Buckfastleigh, the first building known to have been built from the quarries around Church Hill. Photo: Sam Turner, April 2002. (See also fig. 53).

clay pits now lie to either side of both rivers. In fact, this landscape is amongst the most industrialised in all of Devon: where the earth itself has not been dug out, much of the former heathland has been planted with conifers or concreted over for industrial estates.

There are stone quarries in most parts of Devon. Some are small, used only for a few houses or a particular farm. Many have been filled in or used as rubbish dumps, and sometimes they can no longer be detected on the surface. Others lie concealed as hollows in woodland, the angular lines of cut rock faces now softened by mossy vegetation and undergrowth. Elsewhere, though, great cavernous quarries gape to the open sky. At Buckfastleigh, for example, the limestone of Church Hill has been quarried for at least 1,000 years. The first building we know was made from the stone was the church of the Holy Trinity itself (figs 98 & 53). Later, from the 16th century onwards, the stone was still being cut for houses, but also burned for lime to sweeten Devon's acid soils. To the south and east of the church, quarries have bitten chunks out of the original churchyard; to the north, the whole hillside has been blasted away by generations of Buckfastleigh quarrymen.

Some of Devon's earliest mines were sunk on the Bere Ferrers peninsula during the 13th century in search of silver. Later, in the 18th and 19th centuries, the mining techniques developed and employed in west Devon and the Tamar valley led the world. Men from the South West exported their methods around the globe, to countries as far away as Argentina and Australia: the international importance of the region's mining heritage has recently been recognised with the inscription of Cornwall and West Devon Mining on UNESCO's list of World Heritage Sites. Engine houses, spoil heaps and old shafts still provide defining aspects of the area's historic character. We will return to the Tamar Valley and its distinctive historic landscape towards the end of the next chapter.

CHAPTER 5

THE HISTORIES OF LOCAL CHARACTER AREAS

From fields and woods, to quarries and mines: rural Devon is a mosaic of many historic landscape types. In the two previous chapters I described and discussed the principal character types used in the Devon HLC project, and tried to explain why their histories and their historic significance meant I selected them to map out the historic landscape of the county. The HLC was a broad-brush project, so there are bound to be generalisations that some people will find unsatisfactory: certain areas will have been attributed to one 'type' or another in error; in some places a little more detailed research might have revealed interesting stories about a particular place. Fortunately, the HLC now forms part of the County Historic Environment Record, and as such it is not static, not a 'finished' item. Instead it is a project in progress, a database that can be updated to allow for mistakes and to incorporate the fruits of future research.

These caveats aside, I hope that the character types discussed in Chapters 3 and 4 do capture something of the essence of Devon's historic landscape. Like most historic landscape characterisations, the Devon project was designed to reflect the county's particular personality. People who live in Devon, or who have spent much time there, will

Fig. 99.   Aerial view to Dartmoor from the north-east.
Photo: Frances Griffith/DCC, SX87, 14th August 1987.

113

know that the way different character types are intermingled varies in different part of the county. Character types are neither spread randomly across Devon, nor do they appear in the same repeated combinations. In certain areas some types hardly exist: in north-west Devon, for example, there are few orchards of any size; in the South Hams, there is little heathland away from the coast. A drive from the north to the south coast will quickly reveal how building and settlement types, crop regimes, and a whole host of other things vary across the county. Most starkly different is Dartmoor, rising up from a sea of fields like some great moory monster (fig. 99); but in the lowlands too there are significant contrasts between one place and another. As Tom Williamson has written, different agricultural resources lie interdigitated in complex patterns (2002); it is not always easy to understand how and why. This chapter will try to show how we can use the data created for the HLC to help appreciate and understand these subtle patterns.

As we have seen, HLC provides a way of simplifying a very complicated succession of criss-crossing landscape histories into a simpler patchwork of character types. As such, it is one of a growing family of generalisations that have been produced to help us understand the Devon landscape. Landscape architects, ecologists, geologists and agriculturalists have all created characterisations of one kind or another. As with HLC, their aim is generally to reduce the complexity of the landscape to something comprehensible and manageable. Where HLC's particular concern is the historicity of the physical landscape, ecologists might be interested in habitat, or landscape architects in assessing the visual qualities of an area. I will discuss how HLC relates to some of these other approaches below. First, it is worth considering some related research by other historians and archaeologists into landscape regions.

REGIONS AND *PAYS*

Landscape historians in England and other parts of Europe have long realised that individual regions were often associated with particular economic and cultural practices. Such regions are commonly labelled with the French term *pays*. Although it has dropped out of use today, the English equivalent 'countrie' was used as long ago as the 16th century by topographers like John Hooker to distinguish different districts in Britain (Fox 1989). Much historical research into the nature of *pays* has been purely textual, relying on documents such as estate accounts, deeds and probate inventories, which list the belongings of men and women and allow us to interpret how they made their livings from the land. Using these sources, Joan Thirsk created maps of the agricultural regions of England in the 16th and 17th centuries, a formative period for Britain's landscape character (Thirsk 1987). She divided Devon into two broad categories and four regions. The coastal South Hams, the hinterland of Barnstaple and Bideford, and a small strip along the eastern county boundary with Dorset were mapped as 'sheep-corn' country, where the agricultural economy was based on a combination of sheep and arable farming (fig. 100). The rest of Devon (along with Cornwall) was occupied with stock rearing, along with some dairying (Thirsk 1987: 28-9). Thirsk's careful research has been very influential, not least because it provides an accessible national overview (Thirsk 1967). Nevertheless, there are clearly many differences on the ground between regions that look similar at the national scale: thus Westmorland's landscape is quite distinct from Cornwall's, and Northumberland has little in common with Devon.

Detailed analysis of medieval and post-medieval documents by Harold Fox has added detail and definition to the picture provided by Thirsk. He points out that the large farming regions themselves showed signs of internal differences and specialization, with certain regions concentrating on particular products from the later medieval period onwards (Fox 1989). In the South Hams, for example, a range of arable crops were grown in the 14th and 15th centuries including oats, wheat and barley; in other parts of Devon barley was

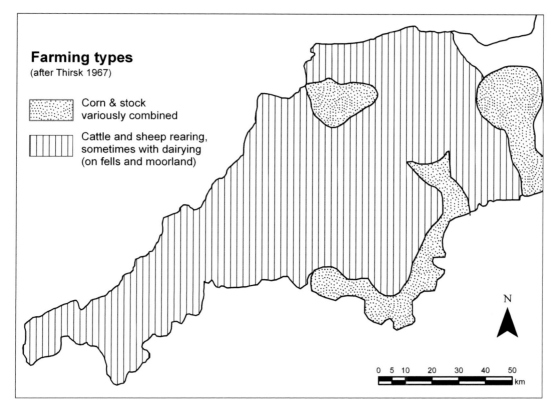

Farming types
(after Thirsk 1967)

Corn & stock
variously combined

Cattle and sheep rearing,
sometimes with dairying
(on fells and moorland)

N

0 5 10   20   30   40   50
km

Fig. 100.   Joan Thirsk's tentative map of the main agricultural regions of Devon
and Cornwall 1500-1640 (based on Thirsk 1967; redrawn by Sarah Lynch).

rare, though rye was often grown in the north and west. Other areas specialised in stock
rearing for external markets. Places like Ashwater in north-west Devon were supplying
the urban centres with meat on the hoof in the 15th century, and in such places 'the very
landscape ... was designed for cattle' (Fox 1995: 128-9). In his earlier work, Fox had already
pointed out how these regional differences in farming practice could be detected in the way
the physical landscape was built. The region around Axminster, for example, was enclosed
early for stock rearing (in the 13th and 14th centuries according to the documents), and
a characteristic pattern of small strip-enclosures with sinuous boundaries was the result
(the 'Strip Enclosures' and 'Enclosures based on Strip Fields' discussed in Chapter 3). By
contrast, much of the South Hams was still farmed as open arable at this time and only
enclosed relatively late in large, regular paddocks like the ones around Stoke Fleming and
Slapton (like Chapter 3's 'Barton Fields'; Fox 1972).

Secondly, Fox has pointed out that the distinctive character of Devon's landscape was the
result of several important phases, not only of developments in the early modern period.
Historians once thought the landscape of the South West was a partly inhabited semi-
wilderness at the beginning of the 12th century, with great blank areas waiting to be cleared
from wildwood by eager pioneers. This old-fashioned view, which was tied closely to the
prevailing opinions of historians all over Europe, was discredited in the later 20th century
through the research of several scholars (Fox 1989: 41-2). They included not only historians
like H.P.R. Finberg, W.G. Hoskins, and Fox himself (Finberg 1953; Hoskins 1963), but also

place-name scholars like Oliver Padel, who established that numerous Cornish settlements still bear the names they were given between AD 500-1100 (Padel 1985). Meanwhile, archaeologists realised that many man-made features in the south-western landscape were already ancient by the end of the Middle Ages, from burial sites and churches to lanes and settlements of all sizes (Thomas 1994; Herring 1986; 2006a). As we saw in Chapter 3, there are many fields on the moors and in the lowlands whose boundaries were first laid out in prehistoric or medieval times.

At a national scale, archaeological research has also highlighted the time-depth of western Britain's so-called 'ancient countryside'. In the 1930s, Cyril Fox drew attention to the differences between the archaeology of Britain's 'highland' and 'lowland' zones (Fox 1938), categories later employed by W.G. Hoskins in his explorations of England's social history (Hoskins 1963). Brian Roberts and Stuart Wrathmell have recently underlined the potential antiquity of the main landscape 'provinces' in England. They suggest that the division between the 'Central Province' (dominated by nucleated villages) and the areas to the south east and west (where dispersed settlement was the norm) could have their roots in the Roman period or even earlier (Roberts & Wrathmell 2000; 2002).

These large-scale changes in the landscape's personality are both intriguing and striking. Nevertheless, more local variations occur across every region of Britain, though they have been studied less and are presently rather poorly understood. Archaeological research into the distribution of different kinds of sites and monuments shows that these regional and local differences may also be long-established: certain kinds of sites are found in some areas and not in others. For example, a recent study for English Heritage's National Mapping Programme showed that prehistoric settlement enclosures are much more common in the Exe Valley than between the rivers Taw and Torridge. The same is true of more recent periods: the HLC shows that catch meadows are far more numerous in the South Hams, the Exe Valley and the southern fringes of Exmoor than elsewhere (fig. 70).

We have already seen that some elements of Devon's landscape have long histories, especially the patterns of fields which are so often closely related to their medieval predecessors. Much that is characteristic of Devon's landscape did emerge in the late medieval and early modern periods, when historians have stressed the emergence of agricultural regions or *pays* in England. But even the most 'ancient' landscape is not the same now as it was 500 or 1,000 years ago, and it is rare to find a landscape whose features all date to the same period. We should not just accept historians' assertions that the 'ancient countryside' has altered little since 1700 (Rackham 1986: 5; Havinden & Staines 1999: 285; *cf.* Turner 2004: 19-20). Plants and trees grow and die, miners and quarrymen come and go, cottages are built and fall down, farmers' methods and markets change: the form of the landscape changes with them. Sometimes great revolutions in technology or attitude transformed people's expectations of the land, resulting in sudden physical alterations; at other times the slow shrinkage of a particular hamlet or the disappearance of a farm has left fields untended for encroaching bracken or furze. Whether changes resulted from a great national movement or a small personal tragedy, they could all affect the landscape in different ways at different times. One thing seems certain: the pace of change and the reasons behind it were rarely the same in every corner of Devon. This is why each region feels slightly different from its neighbour: history's threads are woven like an intricate web across the landscape, and each place has been shaped a slightly different way. The question I want to explore in this chapter is whether the data mapped for the HLC can help us unravel some of these intricacies and take us towards a richer understanding of Devon's historic landscape.

LOCAL HISTORIC CHARACTER AREAS

Landscape historians have identified the emergence of farming regions as a key stage in the creation of today's rural landscape. Their analyses have traditionally been based on historical documents, with occasional forays into the form of the physical landscape led by scholars such as Harold Fox. Archaeologists have tended not to engage with questions about the form of the Devon landscape at the regional scale, preferring instead to generalise from specific sites or well-studied but defined landscapes.

The Devon HLC has characterised the whole county's landscape into different historic landscape types. Because this data has been mapped for the whole county, it ought to be possible to find out whether farming regions can be detected in the post-medieval and modern landscape, and how different character types have interacted to create them. What aspects of their identity do different regions owe to different periods? Did the distinctive aspects of some areas' landscapes emerge earlier than those of others? To what extent does today's landscape reflect the character of earlier times?

To answer questions like these, it was necessary to establish a method for analysing the results of the HLC and picking out repeated patterns and combinations in different regions. To do this, I worked with colleagues at Newcastle University's School of Civil Engineering and Geosciences to create a GIS-based generalisation of historic landscape types. In GIS terms, 'generalisation' is exactly what it sounds: it allows the user to simplify a spatial dataset by filtering out 'noise'. This process leaves a simpler pattern that reveals the distribution of the main components. In the case of the Devon HLC, the 'noise' is provided by small polygons interspersed between bigger blocks of widespread landscape character types. These small polygons often comprised 'minor' character types – for example orchards, quarries, mines and watermeadows – that tend to occupy relatively small areas. However, these are often crucial to the historic character of an areas or place, and they needed to be taken into account in the analysis. So generalising the Devon HLC data was a two-stage process. Our 'First Generalisation' gave us large blocks (some very large) showing which areas were dominated by the commonest historic character types[1]. In some ways, the results were predictable – for example, Dartmoor emerged clearly as an area dominated by rough ground. Elsewhere, though, this First Generalisation already began to pick out smaller areas where the historic character of the landscape related clearly to more subtle landscape histories – for example, showing where the boundaries lay between areas dominated by medieval-derived fields and those with later barton fields in the South Hams (see fig. 5). This shows some interesting similarities to the generalisations produced by other scholars from different sources, for example Thirsk's agricultural regions (fig. 100).

Secondly, we needed to assess the contribution of the 'minor' character types to help divide up the large zones created in the First Generalisation. This was not a straightforward operation in GIS because the historic landscape character of an area might depend on the interrelationships between two, three, or more individual HLC types. We tried various filtering and generalisation techniques, but in the end settled on a compromise between ArcGIS's filters and the human eye. This might seem rather subjective, but in reality all the generalising techniques we used depended on specialist judgement – the user always had to set the parameters for the filter, a process that involved a certain amount of trial and error to create results we felt were appropriate to the data. So in the Second Generalisation, we created a 'centroid' for every polygon in the HLC – a dot showing where its geographical centre lay. For each First Generalisation polygon, we then removed the 'primary' character type (the one that covered the greatest area and to which we generalised in the first stage). This left us with centroids for all the other character types inside each First Generalisation polygon. By displaying this data as centroids with weighted dots or as polygons, it was possible to assess both their frequency and relative area within each First Generalisation polygon. I used them as a guide to split the First Generalisation polygons into smaller

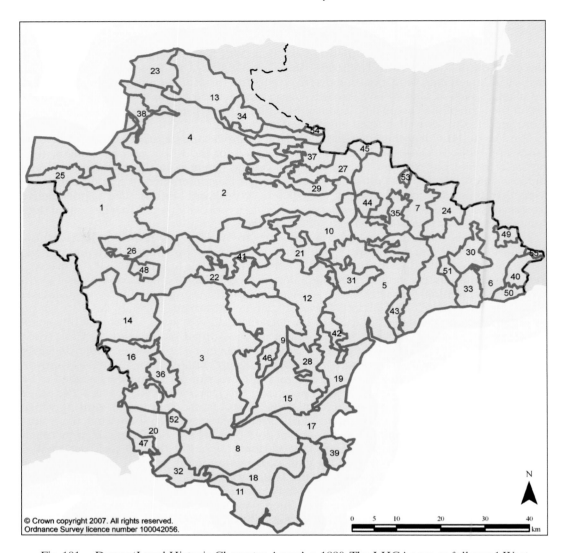

Fig. 101.   Devon 'Local Historic Character Areas', *c.* 1890. The LHCAs are as follows: 1 West Culm, 2 Central Culm, 3 Dartmoor, 4 Taw and Torridge, 5 Lower Exe, 6 Eastern Valleys, 7 Exe and Culm, 8 Upper South Hams, 9 East Dartmoor, 10 Taw and Exe, 11 South Hams Coast, 2 Middle Teign, 13 Exmoor Borders, 14 Upper Tamar, 15 Denbury, 16 Tamar Valley, 17 Torbay, 18 Middle South Hams, 19 Lower Teign, 20 Plym, 21 Crediton Bartons, 22 Whiddon, 23 West Down and Coast, 24 Blackdown Borders, 25 Hartland Moors, 26 Torrington Moors, 27 Iron Mill, 28 Bovey Basin, 29 Witheridge, 30 Blackdown Ridges, 31 Exeter, 32 Yealm Coast, 33 Beer and Blackbury, 34 Exmoor Bartons, 35 Culm Valley, 36 West Dartmoor, 37 Knowstone, 38 Taw Torridge Estuary, 39 Churston, 40 SE Borders, 41 Itton, 42 Haldon Hills, 43 Woodbury, 44 Tiverton Bartons, 45 Morebath, 46 Haytor, 47 Plymouth, 48 Broadbury, 49 Chardstock, 50 Rousdon, 51 Farway, 52 South West Dartmoor, 53 Grand Western, 54 Anstey Commons, 55 Hawkchurch.

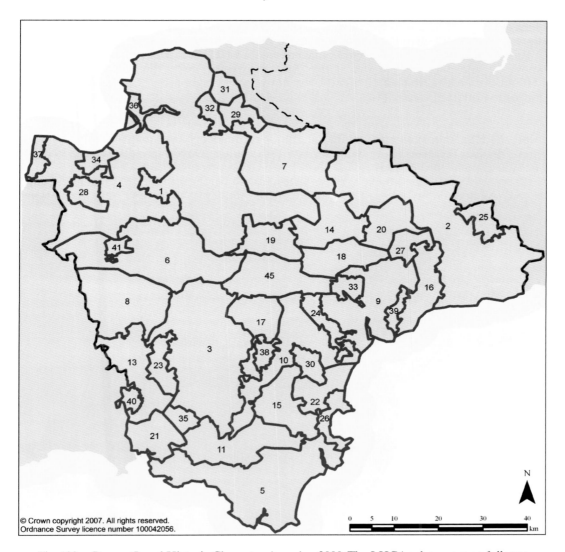

Fig. 102.   Devon 'Local Historic Character Areas', *c.* 2000. The LHCAs shown are as follows: 1 Taw, 2 East Devon, 3 High Dartmoor, 4 North West Devon, 5 South Coast, 6 Mid West Devon, 7 Mid Devon Hills, 8 Wolf and Thrushel, 9 Exe and Clyst, 10 Dartmoor SE Fringe, 11 Inland South Hams, 13 Middle Tamar, 14 Cadbury, 15 Dart Valley, 16 Otter Valley, 17 Dartmoor Farms, 18 Creedy Exe Culm, 19 Copplestone, 20 Cullompton, 21 Plymouth City, 22 Teign and country, 23 Tavy and Walkham, 24 Haldon Ridge, 25 Upper Otter and Yart, 26 Torbay Towns, 27 Yolridge, 28 Waldon and Torridge, 29 Bray, 30 Teign Towns, 1 Bratton Fleming, 32 Yeo and Hutcherton, 33 Exeter City, 34 Parkham, 35 Lee Moor, 36 Rivers and Burrows, 37 Hartland Coast, 38 Eastern Tors, 39 Woodbury Common, 40 Bere, 41 Cookworthy, 45 Yeo and Troney.

blocks characterised by particular HLC types[2]. The result was the Second Generalisation (fig. 101). We have called these 'Local Historic Character Areas' or LHCAs.

This process was undertaken twice: once to create LHCAs for Devon's late-19th century landscape, and once for the end of the 20th century (fig. 102). The number and size of LHCAs for each period differ slightly, but nevertheless comparing the two reveals some interesting similarities.

Historic Landscape Character in the Late 19th Century

Using the HLC data created from the 1st edition Ordnance Survey map and other sources, I have divided the historic landscape of late 19th century Devon into 55 discrete LHCAs. For landscape historians, they reveal many interesting patterns.

Firstly, we can compare them to other historians' and archaeologists' *pays* and landscape regions. As noted above, Joan Thirsk divided early modern Devon into 2 landscape types

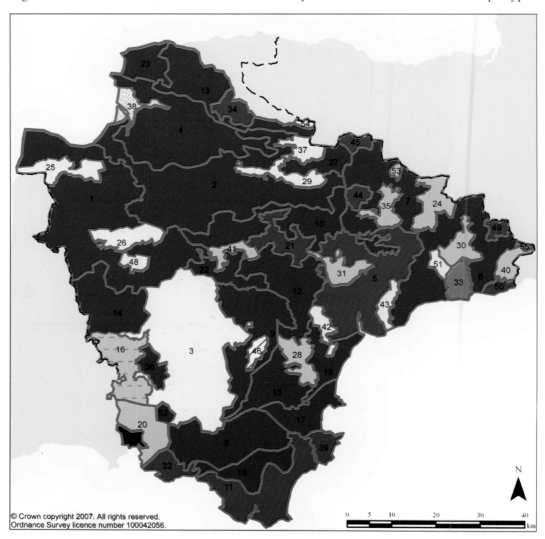

Fig. 103.   The 19th century LHCAs and the dominant HLC type within each one.

and 4 broad landscape regions. These were firstly the 'sheep-corn' country of the coastal South Hams and Exe estuary, the hinterland of the Taw/Torridge estuary, and a narrow strip along the eastern county boundary; and secondly stock rearing with dairying in the rest of the county (Thirsk 1987: 28-9). In broad terms some similar divisions may be reflected in the LHCAs. In particular, the South Hams Coast, Churston and Lower Exe LHCAs match closely one of Thirsk's sheep-corn regions. In the late 19th century all these areas were dominated by barton fields (though Thirsk does not map the break between Brixham and Haldon where barton fields were rare). Likewise the Taw and Torridge LHCA is distinctively different to neighbouring regions, even though it is quite different in its composition to the south coast barton farming areas. The eastern border of the county is divided into several separate late 19th century LHCAs, rather than one homogenous area. Likewise, the rest of the county is split into many separate LHCAs based on its historic landscape character. So as might be expected, Thirsk's research into early modern farming regions and customs appears to correspond in some ways to the physical form of the historic landscape as it survived in the 19th century. However, the LHCAs suggest that detailed research on specific sub-regions would highlight more localised contrasts in farming practice.

The research on settlement patterns by Roberts and Wrathmell provides a more detailed picture of regional landscapes (2000). The maps in their *Atlas of Rural Settlement in England* depict the density of dispersed settlement compared to the frequency and size of nucleated settlements in the 19th century. We might expect settlement form and type to relate to the historic landscape in some way, and indeed there are correspondences between their 'local regions' and the late 19th century LHCAs. Most obviously we can pick out Dartmoor and Woodbury Common on Roberts' and Wrathmell's map as areas with very low settlement densities; they have also been mapped as individual LHCAs. The Yealm Coast and South Hams Coast LHCAs correspond closely to the *Atlas'* South Hams (Coast) local region, with its low levels of dispersed settlement, large nucleations and (from the HLC) large areas of barton fields. In mid-Devon, the Little Dart/Exe Divide local region with low levels of dispersion roughly matches the Knowstone, Iron Mill and Witheridge LHCAs.

There are clearly relationships between landscape character and settlement type. Through future detailed work we will come to understand these better. Roberts' and Wrathmell's research was undertaken at a nationwide scale, and it provides starting points for the examination of local and regional trends. The HLC data records a far greater number of variables and local variations, which makes it a richer quarry for understanding variations in character within individual counties or regions. Fig. 103, for example, shows the 19th century LHCAs and the dominant HLC type in each one, i.e. the type that covers the greatest area within it. As discussed above, just reflecting the dominant type here would not necessarily provide a true reflection of historic character and the subtle variations between areas. LHCAs with broadly similar make-ups often vary in their 'details', and these variations might have given them quite different 'feels' to one another in the past. For example, the East Dartmoor and Denbury LHCAs are neighbours to the south-east of Dartmoor. In the late 19th century, medieval enclosures based on strip fields were the most common HLC type in both areas, occupying 43% of the former area and 71% of the latter. In other ways the two areas were also similar: for example, both had about the same amount of post-medieval enclosures, parks/gardens and conifer plantations. In Denbury, however, there were also significant amounts of orchard (4.6%), whereas there was little of this in East Dartmoor (0.6%). For rough ground and broadleaved woodland, the positions are reversed: only 3% and 4.7% (respectively) of Denbury compared to 26% and 14.3% of East Dartmoor. Because the LHCAs are based on more than just their principal constituent, they can present quite subtle variations in local landscape character. Such differences were undoubtedly important for people's experience of the landscape in the past.

We can also compare the relative proportions of character types in each LHCA to find out which areas are most similar to one another in terms of their overall composition. We

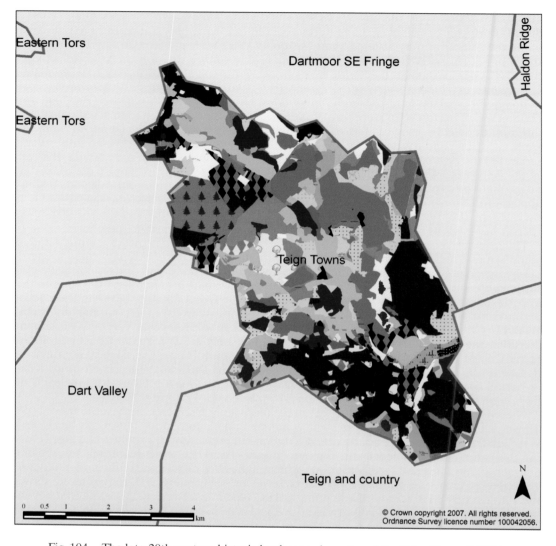

Fig. 104.   The late-20th century historic landscape character of the Teign Towns LHCA.

might expect neighbouring regions to resemble one another more closely than distant ones. In some cases this is true: it was sometimes hard to decide where to draw the line between individual LHCAs, and the 'boundaries' of LHCAs should certainly not be regarded as immovable (e.g. the Central Culm and Taw & Exe LHCAs). Different regions often merge together imperceptibly, and it is probably best to imagine the boundaries between LHCAs as fuzzy lines or border zones[3].

However, it is not only neighbouring LHCAs that share similar characteristics. Some widely separated 19th century regions were composed of very similar mixes of HLC types. Thus the composition of the Denbury LHCA was very similar to that of the Taw & Exe LHCA, over 30km away. They were both dominated by medieval fields based on strip

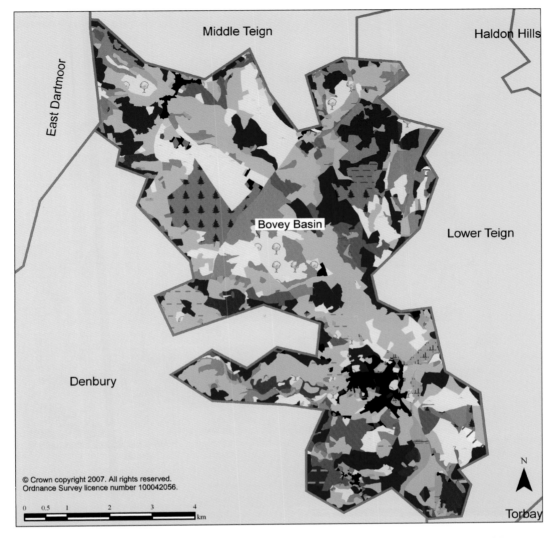

Fig. 105.   The late-19th century historic landscape character of the Bovey Basin LHCA.

fields, and had similar proportions of woodland, post-medieval enclosure, meadow, and other landscape types, the only exceptions being that there were more orchards in the former and more barton fields in the latter. Likewise, Torrington Moors, Hartland Moors and Witheridge were all areas with much rough ground interspersed between medieval enclosures, though there was rather more woodland in Witheridge than the other areas.

Of course, maps of LHCAs do not provide detailed interpretations and explanations for how and why any given landscape came to look the way it did in the past: this requires a further stage of research and interpretation. Nevertheless, LHCAs do at least provide a starting point, and a way to comprehend each landscape's components that has been missing until now.

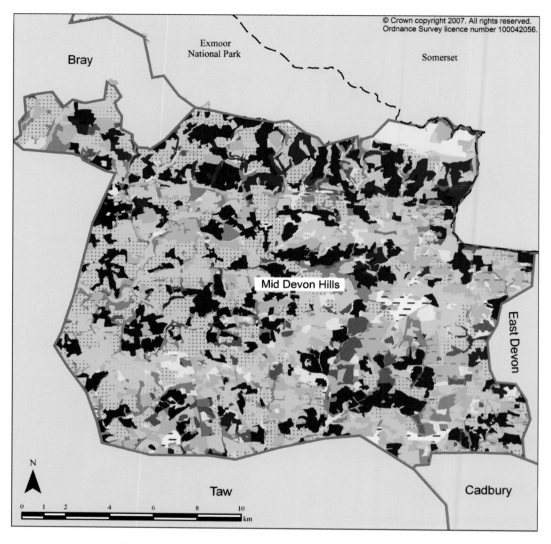

Fig. 106.   The modern HLC of the Mid Devon Hills LHCA.

Local Historic Character Areas at the End of the 20th Century
Using the method outlined above, I have also created LHCAs for the modern landscape.
They show that there have been major changes in the landscape since the 1890s, some of
which have fundamentally changed the character of the countryside. However, the LHCAs
also show that in many areas modern changes have emphasised pre-existing trends and
continued earlier trajectories of change.

I have divided Devon's modern landscape into 41 LHCAs. Some have witnessed
relatively little change since the late 19th century, for example High Dartmoor, Woodbury
Common, and the Tamar Valley. In others, the extent of the LHCA has remained similar,
though its dominant historic character has changed fundamentally. The Bovey Basin/Teign
Towns LHCAs provide a good example. In this area there was a massive intensification

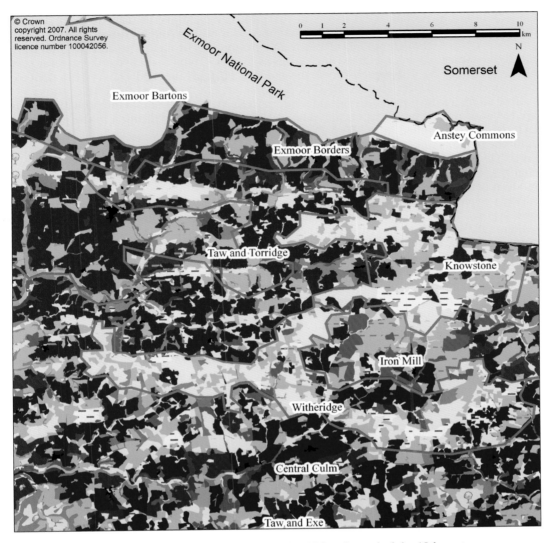

Fig. 107.   The HLC of the area shown in fig. 106 at the end of the 19th century, with LHCAs of *c.* 1890.

of quarrying, industry and urban development in the 20th century (fig. 104). However, we might argue that this change is at least in keeping with *trajectories* established in the post-medieval period and even earlier: quarrying, potteries and other industries formed a significant element of this area's landscape in the 19th century (fig. 105). Of 41 modern LHCAs, 15 are dominated by 20th-century HLC types such as suburban housing, quarrying and other industrial activities, conifer plantations or modern fields.

Elsewhere, the boundaries of modern LHCAs fall along different lines to those of their post-medieval predecessors. At first glance, it seems a little confusing that this has happened where the principal HLC type has remained an ancient one (commonly medieval enclosures based on strip fields). The explanation is normally that several HLC types have been altered within a particular area, leading to a situation where the balance between different HLC types is different now to what it was in the past. For example, in the late 19th century the area of the Mid Devon Hills LHCA comprised a mix of rough ground and medieval enclosures. Most (though not all) of this rough ground was brought into cultivation during the 20th century, leaving medieval enclosures as the HLC type that covers the greater part of the area (e.g. fig. 106, which shows the modern HLC of the Mid Devon Hills LHCA, compared to fig. 107 showing the HLC of the same area at the end of the 19th century).

If we compare the post-medieval and modern LHCAs, we can see that the principal trends are towards amalgamation of earlier character areas and a simplification in the pattern of LHCAs. This is typified in the East Devon LHCA, where around 15 earlier LHCAs now combine to make one large character area. The coherence of the earlier landscape character units has been broken down during the 20th century by piecemeal 'improvements' and changes. Processes such as the enclosure of small parcels of heathland, the growth of modern settlements and the destruction of orchards and historic field boundaries have slowly robbed earlier LHCAs of their former local distinctiveness. These modern processes owe a great deal to developments common on a national scale in farming, industry and settlement. Williamson has stressed the importance of the developing communications network for agricultural patterns in the later post-medieval period (2002). The railways meant produce could effectively be transmitted to its target markets from great distances, and regional patterns emerged which saw the east of England specializing in arable crops and the west in pastoral production. National and international agricultural policy, effective chemical fertilizers, and the long-range markets now available to farmers via the road network have led to more alterations in the farming landscape, often taking it even further from its earlier local character. People commute long distances to work, and can easily live in the countryside and work in town; likewise small business can operate from offices or industrial units based virtually anywhere, thanks to modern roads and communications technology. In terms of local landscapes, the result can be piecemeal changes that have little to do with traditional patterns: hence the erosion of local distinctiveness in the rural landscape.

These processes have led to substantial changes in the distinctive character of some areas. Even so, we should not be too gloomy about the future of Devon's characteristic landscapes. In many places where 'modern' fields dominate, most of the boundaries are in fact post-medieval or earlier: the fields here are only 'modern' in the sense that many *other* historic boundaries have been removed, creating much larger fields than once existed. Of course, this has been highly destructive and measures to preserve historic boundaries must be strengthened to protect Devon's surviving hedgebanks – something the 1997 Hedgerow Regulations have failed to do adequately. It is noticeable that the only areas without major field-boundary loss in the later 20th century lie inside the specially protected perimeter of Dartmoor National Park.

In some ways, the pattern of hedgerow destruction has emphasised pre-existing trends. For example, the biggest fields today are often to be found in the same areas as the biggest fields 120 years ago. In the 19th century, these were often post-medieval enclosures or barton fields (e.g. in the modern Exe & Clyst, Creedy/Exe/Culm, and South Coast LHCAs). They commonly occupied relatively good arable land on fertile soils like the valleys of the Creedy, Exe and lower Dart. In these regions farmers could remove a few ancient boundaries during mechanization after the Second World War and create large, easily-worked arable fields.

On the other hand, the rise of mechanization and intensive farming techniques has lead to large-scale changes that are quite at odds with earlier historic character in many places. Today's Otter Valley, Upper Otter & Yarty, and North-West Devon LHCAs are all good examples of regions once characterised by relatively small, medieval-derived fields that have witnessed massive field-boundary loss in the 20th century. In many places, this has also been accompanied by the destruction of historic farms and settlements (fig. 108).

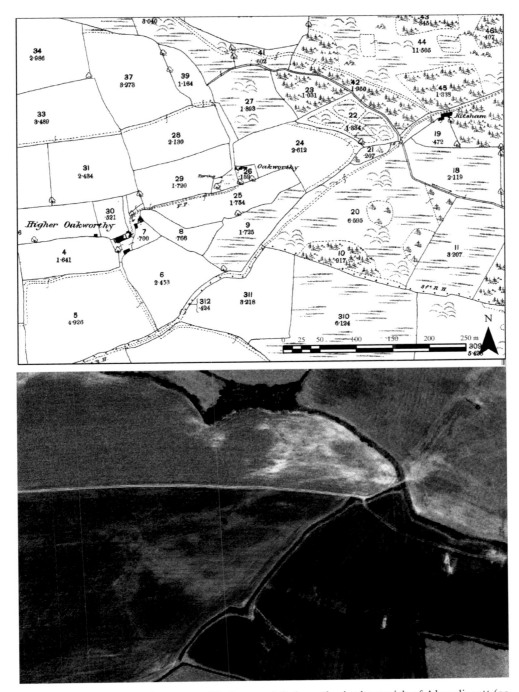

Fig. 108. Top: Three settlements at Kitsham and Oakworthy, in the parish of Alverdiscott (as shown on the 1st edn OS 1:2,500 1887-88). Bottom: the sites of the same three places, all now destroyed and under arable crops, but just visible here as soilmarks or cropmarks. (Photo: © getmapping, 2000. Map: reproduced by kind permission of Landmark, © and database right Crown copyright and Landmark Information Group Ltd (all rights reserved 2007)).

127

LOCAL HISTORIC CHARACTER AND OTHER CHARACTERISATIONS

Academic and professional disciplines such as planning, ecology, landscape architecture and geology have been using characterisation-based approaches for many years. Generally speaking, it can be hard to compare these characterisations to the basic HLC data because they were intended to map larger areas than the original HLC polygons. The Local Historic Character Areas are much easier to compare directly because they tend to be on a similar scale. By doing so we discover that sometimes, though not always, it is clear how the natural geology and environment has influenced the development of patterns in the cultural landscape.

'Natural' Character Areas
In 1996 the Countryside Agency and English Nature published a map with the intention of showing which areas of England shared the same broad character in terms of landscape, wildlife and natural features. The 'Joint Character Areas' map divided Devon's landscape into six principal zones. By comparing the geological map of Devon with these Character Areas, it becomes clear that the basis of what they represent is geology. Thus, the Permian rocks of the Exe Valley correspond closely to the Devon Redlands character area, the granite defines the Dartmoor character area, and the Carboniferous rocks of north Devon and north Cornwall are represented by the Culm character area. These large-scale divisions are hard to relate to historic character areas.

More recently, the Countryside Agency commissioned a detailed landscape character typology based on a range of criteria. These included not only landform and soils, but also elements of the cultural landscape such as landcover (e.g. urban settlement, woodland, farmland of various sorts) and settlement pattern analysis. The aim was to create a characterisation that reflected the ways natural and cultural elements combined in specific areas to create local character (Warnock 2002). To this end, many detailed 'Landscape Description Units' were identified as the basis for larger-scale 'Landscape Character Types,' the equivalent in countryside character terms of our LHCAs. There are about 93 separate areas of these Landscape Character Types in Devon (though some extend across the county boundaries). Some of them match quite closely the localised distribution of particular historic landscape character *types*, especially where local historic land-use is clearly related to soils and topography. The hilltops and valley-bottoms of east Devon are good examples: here, certain 'Landscape Character Types' closely match areas where enclosed fields and conifer plantations replaced open heaths on the high ground during the post-medieval period, and others coincide with large areas of former watermeadow on alluvial deposits along the river valleys. However, relatively few of the Countryside Agency's 'Landscape Character Types' bear close relationships to the LHCAs created for the Devon HLC project. This probably shows that the Countryside Agency gave priority to soils, topography and environment when they were preparing their characterisation, rather than to cultural factors. Indeed, the range of cultural indicators used was limited and tended not to indicate *historic* aspects of the landscape's development. The 'Landscape Character Types' lean towards presenting physiographic zones, whereas the Local *Historic* Character Areas reflect more of the cultural subtleties that result from a long and complex landscape history. These complexities do not relate only to environmental factors, even though soils, rocks, and weather could be very important at different times in different places.

The Physical Landscape: Geology, Soils, Topography
Some recent research suggests the physical environment was the essential factor governing the development of the cultural landscape during the English Middle Ages. In medieval East Anglia, for example, Tom Williamson has argued strongly that different patterns of nucleated and dispersed settlement relate to particular environmental constraints

Fig. 109. The River Torridge at Bideford. The dunes, sand and mud of the Taw and Torridge estuaries give the area a distinctive feel, and have contributed strongly to the development of its historic character. Photo: Frances Griffith/DCC, Bideford old and new bridges, SS4627, 6th August 1985.

(Williamson 2003). Many of the Local Historic Character Areas identified in Devon clearly have direct relationships with the underlying geology and soils. These links were generally clearer in the late 19th century LHCAs than today, perhaps because modern agricultural fertilizers and mechanised techniques have allowed farmers to overcome natural limitations more easily than in the past. Most obvious are the LHCAs dominated by coastal character types, as around Appledore and Braunton Burrows on the north coast, where extensive areas of mud and sand dominate the character of the Taw/Torridge estuaries (fig. 109), but there are also clear inland examples that encompass blocks of particular soil types, for example the Bovey basin with its Tertiary clays in south Devon (fig. 105).

The South West peninsula has a long and complex geological history (recently summarised in Caseldine 1999 and Webb 2006). Geologists have long used characterisation maps to show where different rocks occur, and they show that Devon's underlying rocks fall into three main categories. First, there is the intrusive granite of Dartmoor. Second, south and north Devon are dominated by sedimentary rocks of the Devonian and Carboniferous periods respectively. Finally, in the east there are younger rocks of the Permian and more recent periods. The soils that formed over these rocks bear close relationships to them, although they are also affected by other factors such as topography, climate, rainfall, drainage and human action. Thus Dartmoor's high granite area is typified by two principal soil types: podzolic soils, formed through percolation and leaching of acidic waters, and permanently

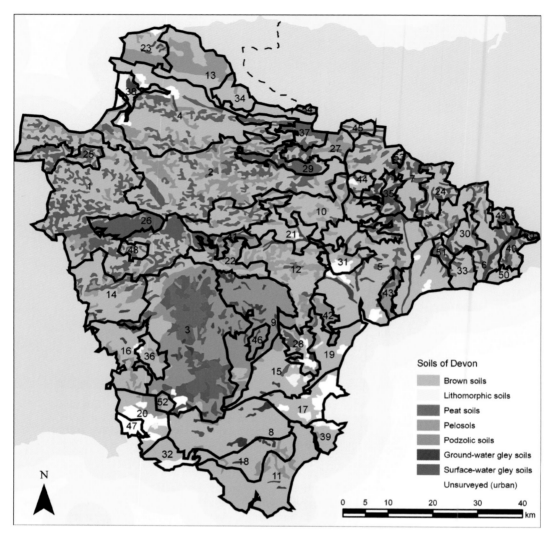

Fig. 110.   Devon soil types with 19th century LHCAs overlain (for key to Character
Areas see fig. 101). (Based on Caseldine 1999: 31, redrawn by Sarah Lynch).

waterlogged peat that formed in the cool, wet conditions after Mesolithic hunters began
clearing woodland margins around 8000 years ago. The relationships between soils and our
LHCAs are sometimes clear. Thus the peat and stagnopodzols that cover most of Dartmoor
underlie the Dartmoor/High Dartmoor LHCAs, whilst the area of brown podzols to the
east closely matches the post-medieval East Dartmoor LHCA (fig. 110). Elsewhere the
form of the cultural landscape in certain small, well-defined LHCAs can clearly be related
to the underlying soils, as on the podzols of the Haldon Hills and Woodbury Common where
heathland and latterly conifer plantation have been the norm. More subtle distinctions are
also detectable. For example, the soils of the large north Devon Central Culm LHCA were
mostly a mixture of brown earths, podzols and surface-water gleys, whereas the West Culm
LHCA to the west was dominated by brown earths and surface-water gleys. The main

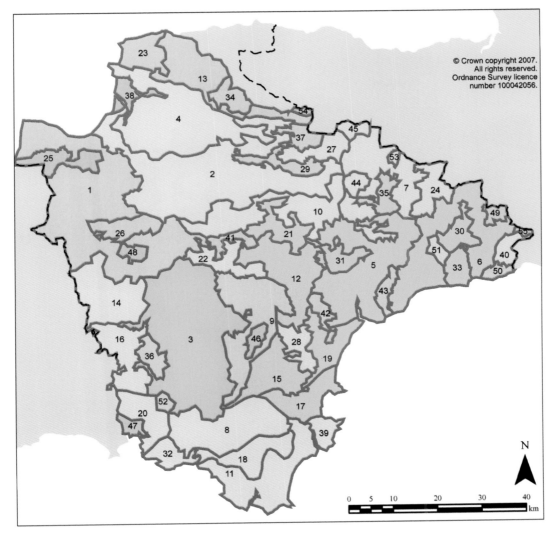

Fig. 111.   Devon LHCAs in 1890 with more than 3% orchard HLC type (pink) and less than 1%
orchard HLC type (blue). For key to numbering of 19th-century HLCAs, see fig. 101.
Source: Devon HLC.

difference between the cultural landscapes of the two areas seems to be that there were
fewer trees (including orchards) and more heaths in West Culm, though this may have been
as much to do with higher rainfall and cooler climate as with soils. These different aspects
must all have interrelated in the past, and for many areas it is hard to pin down specific
individual factors that controlled the development of historic character.

It is undeniable that differences in soils and geology were very important in shaping
the character of past landscapes (Williamson 2003), but they did not entirely determine
the nature of farming and land use (Jones & Page 2006: 95-9; Taylor 2002). Even though
landscape character types like moorland, heath, marsh and woodland are important
habitats for Devon's flora and fauna, we are justified in seeing patterns of these resources

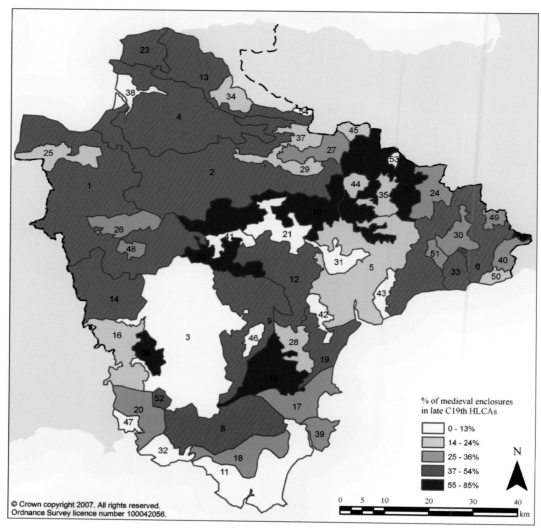

Fig. 112. The percentage of the area of each LHCA (*c.* 1890) occupied by medieval enclosures HLC types. For key to numbering of 19th-century HLCAs, see fig. 101. Source: Devon HLC.

as 'cultural' and using the term 'cultural landscape' to discuss them. In part, this is because people saw them in specifically 'cultural' ways, and attached a range of values to them based on their own perspectives (see e.g. Roymans 1995; Altenberg 2003; Franklin 2006). But we must also remember that as well as being important natural environments, these character types often formed an important part of the local farming economy in the past. Where they existed, it was often because people allowed them to, rather than just because they had no choice in the matter. The heaths and moors could have been ploughed up (Fletcher & Dunn 1999), the trees could have been cut down (Caseldine 1999), and the marshes could have been drained (Rippon 2000). Depending on the technology available to them, people could have changed these land uses in many ways, and the history of post-medieval agriculture shows clearly that they often did (Williamson 2002). In fact, human modification of soils in the South West has a long history: the peats of Dartmoor and the other south-western uplands began to form in part because of tree-clearance by Mesolithic hunters. Unproductive Exmoor podzols have been converted into useful soils in just over a hundred years; in Cornwall, manuring with sea sand, seaweed and other fertilizers during the last 1500 years has created deep man-made soils that can be farmed productively (Webb 2006: 34).

Besides these considerations, we can see that the distribution and combination of historic character types in some LHCAs does not seem closely related to soils or geology. It is not easy to see why the South Hams Coast LHCA (with its expanses of barton fields) was so different to the Middle South Hams (mostly medieval enclosures): both comprise brown earths with similar farming potential, and they overlie similar rock formations. In other places, coherent LHCAs lie across *different* soil types: why, for example, was the western half of the Taw & Exe LHCA more like its eastern half than the neighbouring Central Culm area, with which its soils seem to have more in common? The answers to such problems must lie in a combination of contributory factors, rather than in simple, monocausal explanations.

As with soils, the physical topography, climate and rainfall conditions have significantly affected human settlement. Some LHCAs are obviously linked to topography, such as High Dartmoor, Woodbury and the Haldon Hills. Generally speaking, the higher land is also wetter and colder (particularly in the west), and over time this has affected not only the crops that will grow reliably, but also the kinds of soils that have formed. The occurrence of significant areas of orchards within LHCAs provides a striking illustration. Orchards can be found in virtually every one of Devon's historic LHCAs: those without significant acreages are all highland areas dominated by rough ground like Dartmoor, Haytor, Hartland Moors and Broadbury. The areas with most orchard lie in the east and south of the county, i.e. the drier and warmer areas. The areas with least orchard are all either mostly high ground, or in the cold, wet north and west (fig. 111). On the other hand, the distribution of many character types does not seem to reflect topography to any great extent. The LHCAs with most medieval enclosures based on strip fields seem more or less randomly distributed (fig. 112), and woodland occurs virtually everywhere apart from the highest moors and heaths.

When we are trying to understand the reasons why the cultural landscape has the form it does today, there are many factors we need to consider. Climate, soils, geology and topography were all important. But so were economic factors, social movements, cultural beliefs, and political affiliations. Thus 47% of all the post-medieval parkland occurs within 25km of Exeter. Put another way, 10 LHCAs had parks and gardens as 4% or more of their total area in the 1890s, and all but a couple of them were on the south coast between Dartmouth and Exmouth, or in the Exe valley (fig. 113). This was probably because Exeter was the county town and most important business was transacted there: it suited the local gentry to be relatively nearby. The gentle climate of the south-east coast surely contributed to its development as an area dotted with holiday villas and resorts, but these could only emerge in a particular historical and social context. Similarly, the division between the Tamar Valley and Upper Tamar LHCAs certainly has something to do with the local geology: many of the alterations to the Tamar Valley landscape occurred during the mining boom of the post-medieval period. But in this region, technological advances (in mining, agriculture, and transport), economic changes in markets and social factors – like the availability of labour – were just as important for the developing character of the landscape.

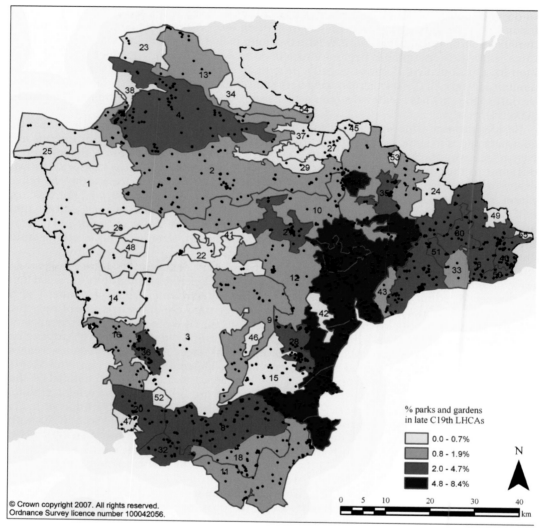

% parks and gardens
in late C19th LHCAs

0.0 - 0.7%
0.8 - 1.9%
2.0 - 4.7%
4.8 - 8.4%

N

0   5   10   20   30   40
km

Fig. 113.   The percentage of the area of each *c.* 1890 LCHA occupied by parks and gardens HLC
type. The black dots show the location of each park or garden. For key to numbering of
19th-century LHCAs, see fig. 101. Source: Devon HLC.

TWO SHORT CASE STUDIES

To understand the development of the cultural landscape, we have to research and
write histories (in the broadest sense) of each place over the long term. By taking an
archaeological perspective on landscape character, we can look at the same places over
long periods and see that there are many ways people might live in and shape a particular
place. In the last part of this chapter, I will illustrate these points in a little more detail
by exploring two distinctive landscapes. Both owe something to the early modern period

when landscape *pays* are thought by historians to have emerged. However, by analyzing the fabric of their historic landscapes we can see clearly how earlier and later periods have also contributed strongly to today's rural environment.

The Tamar Valley

The valley of the River Tamar has a highly distinctive local character. Today its middle section forms an Area of Outstanding Natural Beauty which crosses the river and includes the countryside on both the Cornwall and Devon banks. On the Devon side, the same area broadly coincides with the 19th century 'Tamar Valley' LHCA identified for this project, lying roughly between Dunterton and Endsleigh House in the north and the bottom of the Bere peninsula in the south[4]. The river may divide the two counties administratively, but the landscape of the valley is united by many characteristic features. Although my focus in this short section is the area covered in the Devon HLC, I will also make reference to some examples from the Cornish side of the river (fig. 114).

Trying to use the HLC to help understand what makes the Tamar Valley special highlights both some of its strengths and weaknesses. On one hand, the HLC presents many character types deriving from the industrial era of the 18th and 19th centuries: numerous mines, quarries, settlements, orchards, fields and other features were first created or radically re-shaped during this period. On the other hand, it illustrates some problems associated with using a relatively limited number of sources, and shows how careful we must be when using HLCs to write about places' histories. Reference to a little in-depth research shows clearly that important episodes in a region's history – even its very recent history – can be partly (or even mostly) overlooked if relevant sources have not been used to inform the original HLC mapping.

Fig. 114.   The River Tamar at Horsebridge, looking south. Photo: Sam Turner, July 2006.

Fig. 115.   A Tamar valley view: looking towards Luckett, Stoke Climsland, from the road below
Clitters on Kit Hill, Cornwall. Photo: Sam Turner, July 2006.

If anything, the history of the Tamar Valley owes even more to its geology and climate
than most other parts of Devon. Most famously, its rich reserves of copper, arsenic, silver,
lead, tin, wolfram, and manganese presented opportunities for mining speculators from
the 18th century to the early 20th. The techniques developed here and in Cornwall were
exported around the world, a fact recently recognized by UNESCO, which has inscribed
Cornwall and West Devon Mining Landscape into its list of World Heritage Sites. The
buildings and earthwork remains of these mining ventures still lie scattered across the
Tamar landscape. They contribute very strongly to the area's historic character, even though
they only ever covered a relatively small area of it (fig. 115). Almost as important in historic
terms, the climate of the Tamar Valley is warm and damp with a very long growing season,
which made it an excellent environment for fruit farming and market gardening. Many
orchards still remain, especially on the Bere peninsula, though far fewer survive today than
existed a hundred years ago.

Before considering industrialization and its landscape legacy, we must remember the
contribution of earlier periods to the Tamar landscape. Neolithic and Bronze Age barrows
litter the moors and heaths that fringe the area, and prehistoric field systems have been
identified stretching up onto the edges of Dartmoor and Kit Hill. Iron Age and Romano-
British settlements like the Trendle near Tavistock nestle amongst today's fields, their
boundaries sometimes still preserved in the modern field pattern. We are not yet sure
how much the rural framework of lanes and boundaries owes to this early period. By
analogy with east Cornwall, it seems likely that the basic medieval settlement structure

was established between the 7th and 9th centuries, and that a familiar pattern of hamlets and roads was in existence by the late Saxon period (Turner 2006a). Then, in the middle of the 10th century, we find the first recorded mention of Tavistock Abbey, an institution that played a hugely important role in the Tamar landscape (Finberg 1951; fig. 6). By the time Domesday Book was compiled, the Abbey controlled an estate that stretched across Devon, Cornwall and Dorset, though the core of its lands were in the Tamar valley, including the modern parishes of Tavistock, Gulworthy and Milton Abbot. During the Middle Ages most of the land seems to have been farmed as unenclosed strips, a pattern which was entirely normal in Devon and Cornwall (Chapter 3; Herring 2006a; Finberg 1951: 86-115). However, from the early 14th century onwards there are documentary records of the enclosure of arable fields. As in the South Hams at the same time, the enclosure of arable land into large, regular closes by a major landowner created barton fields like the ones still visible around the abbot's demesne farm at Hurdwick Barton (Finberg 1951: 49-51). These large, regular closes with their slightly curving boundaries are typical of the area to the north and west of Tavistock. Some leases of the time even specify the dimensions of the boundaries being created: a ditch four feet wide and four feet deep next to a bank at Woodovis, for example (Finberg 1951: 50). The character of these Tavistock fields is much the same as enclosures in other parts of Devon where similar agricultural developments were taking place. Elsewhere in the Tamar valley patterns of smaller medieval enclosures show that individual tenants were able to acquire and enclose strips of land, as on the Cornish side of the river around Metherell and Harrowbarrow, or on the Devon side at Bere Alston. These developments of the medieval and early modern periods are quite typical. In this sense, the late medieval and early modern periods witnessed the creation of a recognizably south-western landscape in the Tamar Valley (figs 116 & 117). The highly distinctive character that the area has today was largely a result of later modifications.

Fig. 116.   A view from Whiteford, Stoke Climsland, towards South Coombeshead. The modern wire fences divide up part of a former park; on the hill, the fields are enclosed with curving medieval boundaries. Beyond these, the conifers of Whiteford Plantation have replaced earlier rough ground. Photo: Sam Turner, July 2006.

Fig. 117.   Sheep graze on valley-bottom meadows at Horsebridge in the Tamar Valley.
Photo: Sam Turner, July 2006.

Fig. 118.   Tin-streaming earthworks on the south side of Kit Hill at Fullaford Road, Callington.
Photo: Sam Turner, February 2002.

Fig. 119.   Mine engine-house at Wheal Martha, Luckett. Photo: Sam Turner, 2006.

Even though it was to be several hundred years before they blossomed to create a really strong local character, we might argue that the seeds of the area's particular distinctiveness were also first sown during the Middle Ages. On the Bere peninsula, for example, silver mines were established by the later 13th century, and on the slopes of Kit Hill and Hingston Down medieval tinners streamed for tin ore (fig. 118). Mining continued on a small scale through the early modern period, but it was not until the 18th century that the industry really took off. For two hundred years after 1700, Cornwall and west Devon were at the forefront of the industrial revolution, developing hard-rock mining techniques that were exported all around the world. The Tamar valley, a heavily mineralized area, was fully involved in this industrialization.

Today the valley is littered with the vestiges of the mining era: the ivy-clad chimneys of old engine houses provide unmistakable markers in a landscape still dotted with great mounds of bare, poisonous mine spoil and the earthworks of mining complexes (fig. 119). By the mid-19th century, the area was frantic with industrial activity: for example, the complex of mines at Devon Great Consols was producing more copper by 1850 than any other site in western Europe (Booker 1967: 143-61). Twenty years later, after the copper operation had become less profitable in the face of dwindling reserves and competition from America and

Fig. 120. The site of Devon Great Consols mine: spoil heaps are visible amongst the conifers of
Blanchdown Wood. Photo: Frances Griffith/DCC, SX47 10th July 1996.

Australia, the same mine was producing half the world's supply of arsenic (fig. 120). There
were over 80 mines in the area producing copper in the second half of the 19th century, and
many thousands of people made their livings in mining and related industries. The miners
and their families had to live somewhere, so they built cottages and settlements like Calstock
and Gunnislake. Conditions were poor: disease and infant mortality were rife and houses
were often horribly overcrowded. In and around Tavistock the Duke of Bedford – whose
forefather had acquired the Tavistock Abbey estate at the Dissolution of the Monasteries
– provided land in the 1850s and 60s for the tidy workers' housing that can still be seen in
the town today. Away from his tightly-controlled lands, more ramshackle settlements like
Kelly Bray and Gunnislake grew up on the Cornish side of the river to service the mining
industry (fig. 121). Individual miners also built cottages and smallholdings on the heaths of
Hingston Down, which they surrounded with regular patterns of little fields.

The impact of the 18th and 19th centuries in this area was by no means confined to mining.
Other industrial activities have also left considerable legacies in the historic landscape.
The line of the River Tamar is marked by kilns where limestone was reduced to lime for
agriculture and building (fig. 122). The remains of brickworks lie on both sides of the river,
for example at Chilsworthy, Bailswood and Rumleigh, and paper mills once operated at
Danescombe and Hatches Green. The quarries of Kit Hill provided stone that was once
exported to London and around the world (fig. 123). In addition to the river itself, railways
and canals provided the transport infrastructure that was so crucial in the industrial age
(Booker 1967; fig. 124).

Fig. 121.   The industrial village of Calstock on the Tamar.
Photo: Frances Griffith/DCC, SX4626 26th August 1984.

Fig. 122.   Limekilns at Cotehele Quay in the Tamar valley. Photo: Sam Turner, August 2004.

Fig. 123.   Kit Hill quarry. Photo: Sam Turner, July 2006.

We should remember that this was not only an industrial landscape in the post-medieval period, but also a farming one. Landowners were interested in improving their returns from the land as well as making profits out of what lay beneath. The famous late-18th century agricultural writer William Marshall lived at Buckland Abbey just south of Buckland Monachorum (fig. 64). He conducted various farming experiments here, and the straightened boundaries in the fields around the Abbey bear witness to his improvements. Other landowners also altered earlier fields, with the occasional insertion of catch-meadows or the re-organisation and straightening of field boundaries. In places, altogether new fields were laid out over previously unenclosed heathland, leading to the regular grid-patterns visible on and around Hingston Down or at Heathfield in Tavistock. Plantations of conifers and lines of beeches planted for shelter are characteristic post-medieval features of this landscape. Indeed, the sixth Duke of Bedford is supposed to have refused to grant mining rights in his plantation at Blanchdown – later Devon Great Consols, one of the world's most productive copper and arsenic mines – on the grounds that it would disturb his pheasants (Booker 1967: 145; fig. 120).

The HLC maps reflect many elements of this rich history. Using them, we can pick out various historic landscape character types that bear witness to the improvements and industrialization of the 18th and 19th centuries. It is clear that this era had a fundamental impact on the character of the pre-existing landscape, which had been largely agricultural and rather similar to many other parts of Devon until 1700 (figs 125 & 126). The HLC confirms just how much the Tamar Valley's surviving historic character was formed during the industrial period.

We are presented with several interesting problems by another distinctive post-medieval Tamar industry. In the second half of the 19th century, minerals were not the only marketable

Fig. 124. The River Tamar
near Cotehele, once a busy
industrial waterway.
Photo: Sam Turner, July 2006

commodity being produced in the valley. The area's steep south-facing slopes and warm, moist climate make it an excellent place to grow fruit, a fact recognized since at least the 16th century (fig. 127). By the late 18th century orchards and market gardening land were commanding much higher prices in the land market than ordinary arable (Tamar AONB & Cornwall County Council 2002: 5-7). The HLC of the late 19th century landscape shows that there were once hundreds of small orchards here (fig. 128). We know from written sources that they grew both hard and soft fruit, especially apples and cherries, but also more exotic crops like mulberries, figs, walnuts and plums. After the Great Western Railway arrived at Plymouth in 1849, it became possible to sell fruit from the Tamar valley orchards at the markets of Covent Garden. When the railways were extended into the valley itself, produce could get to London in just one day (Booker 1967).

In the 1860s local entrepreneurs realized that soft fruits like strawberries grown in the Tamar valley were ready several weeks earlier than those from other parts of England. For a few weeks each year they could command premium prices, and the strawberry industry boomed from the mid 19th century until the beginning of the First World War. Other fruits

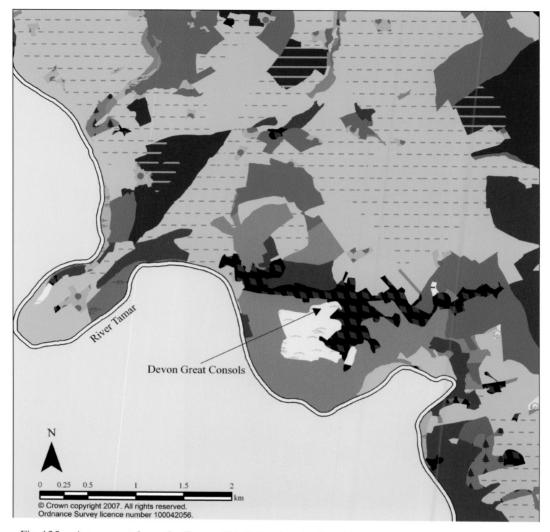

River Tamar

Devon Great Consols

N

| 0 | 0.25 | 0.5 | 1 | 1.5 | 2 | |
km

Fig. 125.   An excerpt from the Devon HLC showing the late 19th century landscape of the Tamar valley around Devon Great Consols. Source: Devon HLC.

were also grown in the area – raspberries, grapes and gooseberries, for example – but strawberries were the principal crop for many years. Along with daffodils, which were grown commercially from the 1880s onwards, they are problematical for the HLC. The sources used for the Devon HLC cannot 'see' soft fruit farming of this sort, except where very small, identifiable closes were specially created – unlike orchards with trees, it was not differentiated on the 1st edition Ordnance Survey maps. It was in fact relatively common for little market-gardening plots to be cleared from rough hillsides – like the ones on the very steep, south-facing valley sides between Cotehele and Calstock – but most fruit-growing was probably in ordinary arable fields. The strawberry industry is therefore largely 'invisible' to a project like the Devon HLC because field boundaries were not modified to accommodate it, and very little trace of it remains in today's landscape. Of course, the methodology could

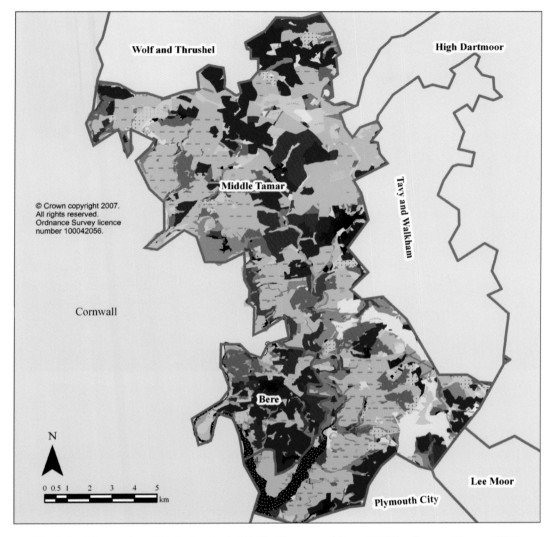

Fig. 126.   The modern HLC of today's Middle Tamar and Bere LHCAs. Source: Devon HLC.

have been adapted to use other sources that do provide relevant information, for example by seeking out relevant maps or by surveying field boundaries for surviving 'escaped' daffodils in spring. Even so, this kind of detailed work can be undertaken more effectively as part of separate research projects whose results can later be integrated with HLC and other datasets *via* the County Historic Environment Record (e.g. Tamar AONB & Cornwall County Council 2002).

The obvious conclusion is that any HLC is only as good as its sources, or at least the interpretations we can reasonably make based on these sources (see Chapter 3). On the Devon side of the Tamar, much of the fruit-growing industry was focused on the Bere peninsula, and several substantial orchards still remain here. Using the HLC we can compare how many orchards have been lost over the last 100 years (fig. 128), but owing to

Fig. 127.   In the orchard at Cotehele in the Tamar valley. Photo: Sam Turner, July 2006.

the nature of our sources we can presently add very little about the history of the strawberry or flower-growing industries in the 19th and 20th centuries.

Eastern Dartmoor

The LHCAs created for both post-medieval and modern Devon divide the eastern part of Dartmoor into two principal regions (fig. 129). Firstly, there is the area of eastern upland centred on Haytor and Ripon Tor. Today, this stretch of moorland is home to few people, but its most important distinguishing feature is abundant archaeological evidence for past cultivation and settlement in the form of earthworks and drystone structures amidst the moorland (the post-medieval LHCA is called 'Haytor'; the modern LHCA 'Eastern Tors'). Secondly, there is an area characterised most strongly by small, scattered farms and their tiny medieval fields ('East Dartmoor' in the post-medieval LHCA; 'Dartmoor Farms' modern LHCA). It would be foolish to claim that the area is just the same now as it was a hundred years ago, since there have been some important changes. These include the decline of moorland industries, the creation of some conifer plantations, the metalling of roads and tracks, and the construction of new houses, farm buildings and tourist facilities. Nevertheless, eastern Dartmoor has maintained more of its traditional, pre-modern character than almost any other inhabited area of Devon. In part, this must be related to the establishment of the Dartmoor National Park in the 1950s and its successful efforts to control the impact of modern life through the planning process. The only really significant modern changes in the farming landscape are to be found in parts of Buckfastleigh and Dean Prior parishes,

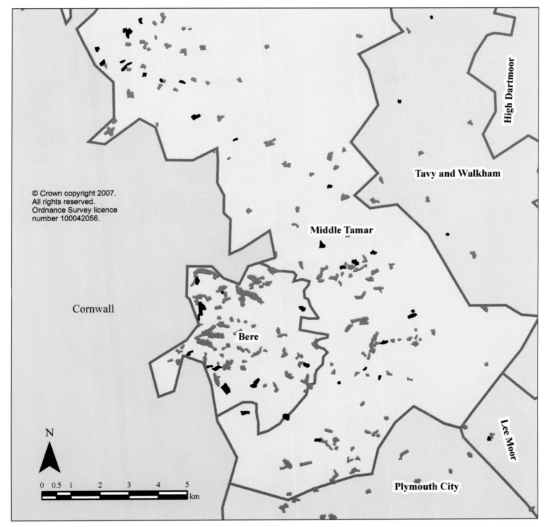

Fig. 128.   The loss of Tamar valley orchards in the 20th century, showing both orchards that survive
from the 1890s (black) and those that have been destroyed (red) against the modern LHCAs.
Source: Devon HLC.

where arable farmers have swept away earlier field boundaries to create massive, machine-
friendly fields. This development largely accounts for the changes in shape of the Dartmoor
LCHAs between the modern and post-medieval periods (figs 101 & 102).

   Today, the historic landscape of eastern Dartmoor comprises great tracts of moorland that
rise above valleys filled with small fields and scattered farms. The boundaries of the fields
are often massively constructed in earth, and stone facings to one or both sides are fairly
common. Although the moorland soils tend to be acid podzols, long centuries of cultivation
have created deeper, more productive soils on the valley slopes. Around the margins of the
moor, especially in the valleys of the major rivers, this farmland gives way to woodland on
the steep lower slopes. There are large areas of plantation in some places, such as Ausewell

147

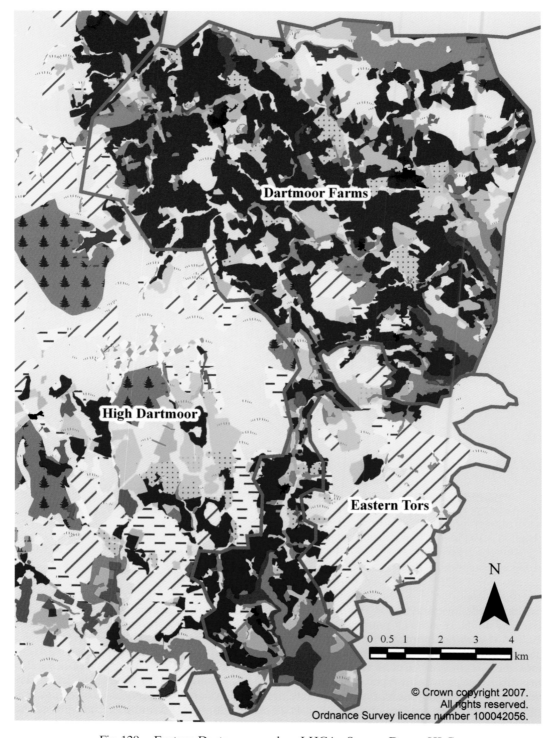

Fig. 129.   Eastern Dartmoor: modern LHCAs. Source: Devon HLC.

Fig. 130.   Tunnaford Farm, looking west towards Fernworthy, Dartmoor, 1976.
© Chris Chapman, used by kind permission.

Common and the valley of the River Webburn, and scrubby recent growth in others; but elsewhere ancient oak woods many centuries old stretch out along the valley sides.

It is not only the modern era whose effects have been relatively slight on eastern Dartmoor: the impact of the post-medieval centuries was also limited. There were changes of course, but compared to other parts of Devon they did not significantly alter the character of the countryside. In the farming landscape, some fields had boundaries straightened and occasionally new farms were created, as at Grendon in Manaton parish. Nevertheless, the area did not witness the kind of large-scale improvements visible on the high moors near Princetown. The 18th and 19th centuries saw a revival in Dartmoor's mining industries, and newly-developed shaft mining techniques were used to exploit the upland mineral reserves. Even so, this industry was focused on relatively few mines, and compared to their medieval antecedents their impact on the Dartmoor landscape was relatively limited, particularly on the eastern side of the moor (Gerrard 1994, fig. 15). The post-medieval industrial developments with the greatest impact on historic landscape character in this area are perhaps those around Haytor, where a granite tramway serviced major stone quarries (Gerrard 1997). Compared to the great quarries and mines of south-west Dartmoor, the Tamar Valley and Cornwall, however, these were fairly small-scale operations. Perhaps most significant was the construction of new buildings. Although we know from excavations that medieval farms did have some outbuildings, most sheds, animal houses and barns on the moor belong to the 18th and 19th centuries (Thorp & Cox 1994). New houses and cottages were also constructed, often in the vernacular tradition but sometimes in more fashionable styles: witness the railway architecture of Holne Chase and the Victorian hamlet of Leusdon, complete with its 19th-century Anglican church.

Fig. 131. Oldsbrim Cross, near Poundsgate.
Photo: Sam Turner, April 2000.

The HLC maps suggest that the essential historic character of eastern Dartmoor owes much more to its prehistoric and medieval past than to these recent periods. We know from numerous archaeological studies what medieval farms and fields looked like on this part of Dartmoor. Detailed archaeological surveys of partially or wholly deserted fieldscapes like those of Holne Moor or Challacombe allow us to identify with some confidence how the medieval fields on the moors developed (Fleming & Ralph 1982; Pattison 1999; figs 18, 26, 48 & 89). We can draw quite safe analogies between the cornditches and fieldbanks of these places and the ones that are still farmed today. Based on these, we can certainly say that most of the fields in the eastern Dartmoor area were probably enclosed well before AD 1500, and that they perpetuate the medieval landscape divisions (fig. 130). So in this region it is not only the framework of today's countryside that is essentially medieval in character, but also the detail. The boundaries have certainly been maintained and repaired in more recent times, but this has usually been done in a way that is consistent with their traditional, ancient form. In such a conservative environment it is perhaps not surprising to find that many late medieval houses still stand around the eastern fringes of the moor. We know from excavations like those at Houndtor, Hutholes and Dinna Clerks what Dartmoor farmhouses of the 13th and 14th centuries were like (Henderson & Weddell 1994); though they are often larger and have normally been embellished since their original construction, standing houses of the 15th and 16th centuries like Sanders, Ollsbrim, Corndon Farm or Uppacott are very much in this medieval tradition (Beacham 1990: 54-7). Devon as a whole is rich in late medieval rural buildings (Child 1990), and with its numerous longhouses, the eastern edge of Dartmoor has more than almost any other region. This abundance extends to other types of surviving medieval monuments too, like the wayside crosses that once gave succour to Christian travellers in the bleak and frightening wilderness of the moors (figs 1, 131 & 132). In the HLC, this medieval character is strongly reflected by the dominance of medieval enclosures in the characterisation, which still comprise over 47% of the Dartmoor Farms LHCA. By comparison, post-medieval field types (including barton fields) make up just over 6% of the same area.

The next most common character type here is the rough ground. It forms the vast majority of the Eastern Tors LHCA, but also a significant proportion of the Dartmoor Farms area. The changing exploitation of the rough ground provides an important theme in the farming history of this region (Fox forthcoming). In terms of its historic character, the frequent patches of rough ground interdigitated with ancient fields and woodlands create a highly distinctive landscape (figs 129 & 130).

Fig. 132.   Middle Bonehill farm, Widecombe, Dartmoor, 1983.
© Chris Chapman, used by kind permission.

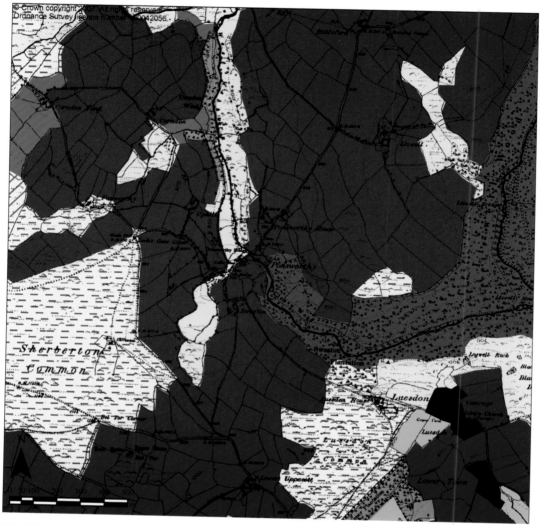

Fig. 133   The historic character of part of the East Dartmoor LHCA, c. 1890. The only significant change here since then – apart from the surfacing of most of the roads and the spelling of 'Leusdon' – has been the growth of scrubby woodland in the valley of the Webburn. 1st edn OS 1:10,560 map, 1886-91. Map reproduced by kind permission of Landmark. © and database right Crown copyright and Landmark Information Group Ltd (all rights reserved 2007).

On the eastern fringes of the moorland, there is little rough ground that has not been affected by farming or industry in the past. The result is that almost everywhere we can detect the remains of prehistoric and medieval farms, mines, quarries and houses (see Chapter 4; figs 86, 87, 93–96). Most commonly, they survive as low earthworks or tumbled stone walls. Detailed archaeological fieldwork, like that of the English Heritage Exeter Survey Office, can unpick these ancient remains and help us explain how they developed (e.g. Pattison 1999). Particularly in winter, when the bracken has died down and the bones of the landscape are laid bare, they contribute strongly to the historic character of this area.

By presenting this data as a map, the HLC can help us understand how all these character types interact to create the particular historic character of the eastern Dartmoor area. It is very clear that the landscape here is one that owes a great deal to the distant past: the remains of prehistoric settlements, farms, burial sites and ritual monuments still dominate much of the rough ground. The way medieval farmers used the land was influenced by the distant past, and they often followed the patterns of boundaries established by Bronze Age people a couple of thousand years earlier (Gerrard 1997). But the most important legacy here is from the Middle Ages (fig. 133). Most of the physical features of today's landscape – the field boundaries, roads and tracks, earthwork remains in the moorland, even many of the standing houses – were already present at the end of the Middle Ages. The extra protection granted to this area by Dartmoor National Park has helped preserve this particular historic character through the upheavals experienced elsewhere in the later 20th century.

ENDNOTES

[1] To make our First Generalisation, we created a raster dataset from the vector polygons, and then applied a 'majority filter' in ArcGIS. We then converted the results back into polygons to give us a new coverage consisting of larger blocks.

[2] This too was a 2-stage process, undertaken first for 'major' components, and second for 'minor' components. The division was necessary because some HLC types tend to occur in small blocks that might otherwise be overlooked, but still make a significant contribution to landscape history and character, one that is often disproportionate to their area. 'Major' components included: Medieval Enclosures; Post-Medieval Enclosures; Rough Ground; Ancient Woodland; Other Woodland; Conifers (and their respective variants). 'Minor' components were: Orchards; Watermeadows (all periods); Industrial/Mining/Quarrying; Parks/Gardens; Settlements; Horticulture.

[3] Sometimes the 'right' place to draw the boundaries between LHCAs was clear: where the East Dartmoor LHCA changes to Haytor, for example, or where the Haldon Hills meets the Lower Exe and Lower Teign.

[4] The late 20th century LHCA map divides the area into the 'Middle Tamar' and 'Bere' LHCAs.

CHAPTER 6

THE LANDSCAPE OF DEVON IN THE 21ST CENTURY

DIRECTIONS OF CHANGE IN THE 20TH CENTURY

The characterisation presented by the Devon HLC stresses the historic dimension of the cultural landscape. But this characterisation of late 20th century Devon is not a map of something that has been destroyed or disappeared. Instead, it is a representation of the modern landscape: the setting for people's lives, work, journeys, holidays, weekend trips and days out. As far as possible, the modern HLC tries to represent a living landscape.

Because the Devon HLC also mapped the historic character of the late 19th century landscape, we can compare the characterisations of the two periods and get some idea of the trajectories of change that have affected rural Devon over the last hundred years. Had we used more 20th century sources – Ordnance Survey maps of the 1950s or 60s, for example – it might have been possible to tie these processes down in more detail. Indeed some recent HLC projects have been attempting to do this, but in Devon we reluctantly decided it would be too time-consuming to introduce another layer to the characterisation. Even so, it is still possible to identify significant trajectories in the development of Devon's landscape by comparing the characterisations of the late 19th and late 20th centuries.

In terms of the area affected, the most widespread alteration has been the removal of old field boundaries. In some places, these have been replaced with modern boundaries like barbed wire fences, but most commonly the old Devon hedgebanks have been removed to create large enclosures that are friendlier to modern agricultural techniques than their predecessors were. The reasons for this trend were many and varied, resulting partly from the influence of government agricultural policies, partly from changing market opportunities, and partly from farmers' perceptions of the best and most modern ways to manage their land. The result was the destruction of thousands of kilometres of hedgebanks between the 1950s-80s, many of them dating back to the Middle Ages. The last decade of the 20th century saw the introduction of financial incentives under the Countryside Stewardship and Evironmentally Sensitive Areas (ESA) schemes whose aim was to encourage farmers to manage hedges sensitively and re-plant grubbed-out stretches. In addition, the Hedgerow Regulations of 1997 and 2002 brought hedges into the realm of planning, and made it more difficult for landowners to destroy them. Although these measures have greatly slowed the removal of hedgebanks, anecdotal evidence suggests considerable stretches are still being destroyed illegally each year (fig. 134) – and the legal removal of small stretches for pipelines, gateways and small developments is also having a significant detrimental effect.

Other modifications have affected much smaller areas, though their effect on the distinctiveness of Devon's landscape character has still been very significant. Orchards provide an excellent example. Apple and other fruit trees were an extremely common sight around Devon farms and villages in the later 19th century, and considerable fruit-farming industries once existed in places like the Tamar Valley, the Dart Valley and parts of east Devon. As mentioned in Chapter 4, the number of fruit trees declined rapidly in the second half of the 20th century, so that few regions now boast significant areas of orchard. As with old field boundaries the reasons for this change were complex, but the result has undeniably been a significant impoverishment of Devon's historic rural landscape. The fragrant spring blossom of remaining orchards in places like the Dart and Tamar valleys reminds us of a rich heritage now lost to much of the county.

The little patches of rough ground that were once so common in much of north and east Devon present a similar story, though in this case 18th and early 19th century records show us that their 'improvement' has a long history. The ideological impetus to make fruitful land from 'waste' was a potent driving force, particularly when combined with a buoyant market for arable produce in the early 19th century and the increasing availability of chemical fertilisers from the 1830s (Turner 2004; Williamson 2002: 140). Though the recessions of the later Victorian period and the interwar years saw much abandonment here, the mechanisation and industrialisation of agriculture since the 1950s has once again made it possible to farm this rough ground profitably. Air photographs can show us where ridge and furrow or other earthworks have been removed by renewed ploughing in the last 50 years – destroying remains that had probably survived from the Middle Ages in many places. Research for the national Mapping Programme has recently identified good examples in several parts of Devon, for example just south of the parish boundary between Northlew and Highampton, between Wagaford Water and Birchen.

Fig.134.   The line of a grubbed-up hedge in the Dart valley, now replaced with a wire fence. The same boundary is visible on fig. 13, extending ENE from the point where the double-hedged lane turns a right-angle to run NNW (close to where the number '440' is marked on fig. 16).
Photo: Sam Turner, July 2006.

The fact that the enclosure and farming of rough ground was well underway by the middle of the 18th century illustrates an important point about these changes: they are all part of the ongoing history of the landscape. We should not simply condemn them just because they disrupt the old arrangements. Change is a constant feature of landscapes, and if we are realistic we have no choice but to accept it. The problems facing us are to work out how we should manage and guide these changes best, what we want to keep or restore and what we are prepared to lose, and whose priorities and agendas we should follow in making these decisions. I will return to these themes towards the end of this chapter.

Furthermore, the story of the rural landscape is by no means only about loss. This is particularly clear in the case of woodland. The deliberate plantation of conifers and other woods, and the creeping growth of scrubby woodland in neglected fields and under-grazed hillsides means that there are far more woodland trees in Devon today than at any time in the last several hundred years – and perhaps twice as much as in the mid-19th century (see Chapter 4). A significant issue here is not quantity, but quality: conifer plantations do not provide very rich habitats, and the well-managed historic woodlands that prevailed in the early 1800s are now often neglected and tangled. The public perception that we need to plant more and more trees is surely a result of successful lobbying efforts by environmentalists – something that those of us concerned to manage and look after the historic cultural landscape would do well to emulate in our own sphere.

Changing Local Character in the 20th Century

Not every part of Devon has been affected equally by the changes of the 20th century. This becomes clear if we use the HLC to assess the degree of landscape change in specific Local Historic Character Areas. Perhaps unsurprisingly, the areas that have witnessed least change in the 20th century mostly lie within Dartmoor National Park (figs 66, 129 & 133). In both the High Dartmoor LHCA, and the other character areas that lie within the Park boundary – Dartmoor Farms and Eastern Tors to the east of the high moor, and Tavy and Walkham to the west – there has been relatively little disruption to the historic cultural landscape over the last 100 years. We might suggest two main reasons for this. Firstly, Dartmoor is a wet and often cold upland area. Although it has witnessed significant arable production in the more distant past, this element of its farming economy has been less important in recent centuries. Compared to neighbouring regions of lowland Devon, relatively few field boundaries have been removed here to cater for the mechanisation of arable production – though there are a few examples in parts of Dean Prior and West Buckfastleigh. Secondly, National Park authorities are able to enforce stricter planning controls than most other planning authorities: this has the effect of limiting development and conserving existing landscapes. Dartmoor National Park was one of the first to be established in the UK under the 1949 National Parks and Access to the Countryside Act (Garrod & Whitby 2005: 220-8). This planning regime, whose provisions for cultural heritage were strengthened in 1995 under the Environment Act, has had a significant impact in protecting landscape features. Even so, Dartmoor has not been immune from 20th century changes. Some major alterations, like the establishment of conifer plantations, antedate the establishment of the National Park in 1951. Even after this, the new planning regime was rather toothless for many years in the face of large-scale infrastructure projects. For example, the Meldon Reservoir drowned a significant area of moorland in the early 1970s, and the A30 dual carriageway – not opened until 1988 – cut right across the northern edge of the Park (DNPA 2004).

Compared to Dartmoor National Park, most other parts of Devon have seen far more landscape change over the last hundred years, and some have changed utterly. Perhaps the greatest changes are to be seen where extractive industries gouged great quarries out of land, like the china clay works on the south-western fringes of Dartmoor. In places such extractive industries have combined with other 20th-century developments to create mixed but largely modern landscapes. The Teign Towns character area is one such place (figs 104

Fig. 135.   A Dart valley view: looking north into Staverton parish. The large fields on the hills in the distance show where historic field boundaries have been removed, mostly since 1950.
Photo: Sam Turner, July 2000.

& 105). Here we can see clearly how the landscape has been transformed by the growth of Newton Abbot and Kingsteignton, the excavation of enormous clay pits along the Teign valley, the plantation of conifers over most of Bovey Heath and the establishment of a huge industrial estate at Heathfield. Elsewhere, of course, the growth of towns and villages has continued a process that began in the 19th century. Suburban dwellings now spread out far across the hills beyond the Victorian villas of Torbay, and cities like Plymouth witnessed exponential growth after World War II.

Whilst change may not have been as radical as this elsewhere, the HLC shows how other developments have influenced the rural landscape. These are typified by two processes: changes in land use and the removal of old field boundaries. Large areas of rough ground have been brought under arable cultivation since 1950. Mechanisation and the availability of effective chemical fertilisers have made it much easier to use land that was previously difficult to cultivate. This is especially noticeable on the Culm Measures of north-west Devon where extensive tracts of rough ground on hill tops and in valley bottoms has been brought under the plough. Elsewhere, landowners and governments have tried other strategies to make use of the heaths and uplands: hence the plantation of Haldon and Cookworthy with conifers. Field boundary loss, though commonly related to such changes of use, has had widespread and severe repercussions. From the South Hams and the Dart Valley to North West Devon, thousands and thousands of kilometres of ancient boundaries were destroyed between the 1950s and 1990s (figs 66 & 135).

Change of one sort or another has long been a characteristic of some Devon landscapes. For example, we might argue that the modern industrialisation of the Bovey Basin-Teign

Towns area makes sense in landscape terms, since there has been significant industrial development here since the 19th century and before. Change could be seen as an integral part of this area's character. Elsewhere, however, long-term stability is much more typical. Dartmoor is distinguished amongst European landscapes because it preserves massive tracts of prehistoric field remains; their survival is a direct result of the way the moors have been used during the intervening three millennia. Rapid change is not a characteristic of Dartmoor's landscape, and we might therefore argue that strict planning controls to preserve it are entirely appropriate. The problem is that we presently have few ways to assess the qualities of more dynamic and more ordinary landscapes, and little understanding of how they are valued by the people that live and work in them. This affects our ability to manage such landscapes and to plan what changes to make or allow in the future.

PARTICULAR THREATS IN THE 21ST CENTURY

Even outside the National Parks, much of Devon's rural landscape is now covered by designations of various sorts that limit development through stricter planning controls. These include Areas of Outstanding Natural Beauty, Sites of Special Scientific Interest, National Nature Reserves and Conservation Areas. Within such areas, the main problems for planners are to decide what kind of developments are appropriate; many of the designations relate to the 'natural' environment, and 'cultural' or 'historic' features may still suffer as a result.

Despite the proliferation of area-based designations, a huge amount of Devon's rural landscape receives no special consideration under the planning system. It tends to be these undesignated zones that face the greatest threats from unsympathetic change and development. Projects like the HLC are intended to highlight the value in these 'ordinary' cultural landscapes, not only in terms of the histories they embody, but also as the setting for people's everyday lives.

The immediate threats of the 21st century can perhaps be divided into two main areas relating to agriculture and urbanisation/industrialisation. Other factors may also be important in the longer term, and we should remember that global issues like climate change may affect Devon's rural landscape too – our low-lying estuaries and coastlines face real risks from flooding and erosion, and in the future changes in plant communities could severely affect Devon's historic character. These are terrible dangers, but we must not allow the threat of them to distract our attention from changes of a more everyday kind.

In farming, mechanisation and monocultures still present risks for our rural landscapes. Even with revised hedgerow regulations in place to protect historic boundaries, the mechanisation that inevitably accompanies modern farming will mean hedgebanks are destroyed and gateways widened to permit access. Changing crop regimes not only lead to changing field systems, but they also change the character of the rural landscape. Over time, such innovations may be accepted: after more than a hundred years, oil-seed rape has become a familiar part of the rural scene. But other new crops could have an even greater impact in the future. Incomes from cereal farming are expected to fall in coming years (Robbins *et al.* 2006: 8), and farmers may turn to new crops. For example, it had been proposed that much of mid and north Devon could be planted with miscanthus (elephant grass) to feed a possible biomass power station at Winkleigh. A plant like elephant grass would tower above the ancient hedgebanks and could completely alter the character of many rural areas.

Over the next fifty years Devon also faces significant urbanisation, industrialisation, and the provision of infrastructure to support these developments. Specific sites like the proposed power stations at Winkleigh and Langage or the expansion of Exeter Airport pose threats not only to the natural environment but also to the historic landscape. Linear projects such as roads and gas pipelines will cut across the grain of the old field systems and disrupt the historic pattern (fig. 41). Urban and industrial sprawl continues to affect not only the margins of existing towns and cities, but also wholly undeveloped sites like the planned new town of Cranbrook along the Roman road between Broadclyst and Rockbeare in east Devon.

CURRENT APPLICATIONS OF HLC

The HLC is intended to help us plan for these challenges with the cultural landscape in mind. It is presently being used for a range of applications in research, management and planning – to help understand and deal with the landscape of the past, present and future (for a more detailed discussion, see Clark *et al.* 2004).

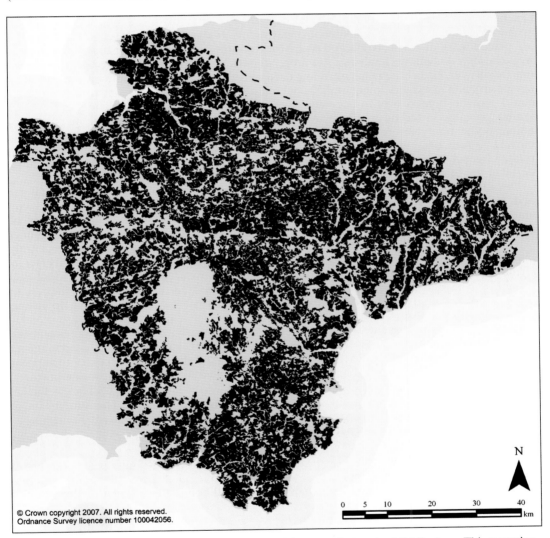

Fig. 136. Areas of Devon probably farmed for arable crops during the Middle Ages. This tentative map shows all areas where surviving or mapped field boundaries or earthworks suggest strip field arable agriculture once took place. Source: Devon HLC.

159

Research

For archaeological research, HLC can help us understand past landscapes – how they were structured, used, and understood by previous generations. In Chapter 3 and 4 I discussed how we can map landscape character types that reflect particular types of land use in the past. For relatively recent periods, we can normally build up quite a detailed impression of what the countryside was like – as with the characterisation of the 19th century landscape in the Devon HLC (see e.g. Turner 2004). Even for more ancient times, the HLC can help us understand factors like the organisation of agricultural resources and their relationships with settlements, churches and other ancient sites (Turner 2006a; fig. 136).

Management

The main uses of HLC are in landscape management and planning. Because the technique has been developed by archaeologists, it is most commonly used at the moment by archaeology and historic environment departments. Inevitably, this affects the values that are placed upon different landscape types: for example, most archaeologists tend to regard well-preserved medieval landscapes as more 'important' than well-preserved post-medieval ones. However, HLC is increasingly being used outside archaeology to help inform decisions by countryside managers in general; the technique's total coverage and flexibility means it could provide a good way to accommodate debates and manage conflicting ideas about landscape value in the future. Finding agreement on priorities for landscape management amongst the many interested parties is difficult, and even to communicate effectively between them presents significant problems. HLC can help with this by providing a relatively easy to understand, geographically-based framework that presents considerable detail at the local level.

Deciding which criteria should be used to judge particular landscapes for management and planning purposes is far from straightforward. Should we preserve typical Devon landscapes or save rare survivals? Is it more appropriate to protect wholly intact areas, or actively re-create lost features? When 'natural' and 'cultural' priorities come into conflict – for example where arable land provides a habitat for rare species, but where arable farming is destroying rare archaeological features – which should take priority? It is virtually impossible to lay down hard-and-fast rules in these areas, and each individual case should be considered and debated on its own merits. The HLC cannot provide answers to these problems, but it can supply information about local historic landscapes to help inform discussion and debate.

In landscape management, HLCs have been used routinely to inform agri-environment schemes for some years now (Clark *et al.* 2004: 13-20). In 2005 the Department of Environment, Food and Rural Affairs (DEFRA) reformed the existing schemes to support farmers' environmental management in England into two new schemes now administered by Natural England, 'Entry-Level' and 'Higher-Level Stewardship' (ELS/HLS – OELS (Organic Entry-Level Stewardship) is available for organic farmers). The stated aim of these schemes is specifically to promote sensitive environmental management. For example, the Entry Level scheme is designed to:

- Improve water quality and reduce soil erosion – by encouraging management which can help to meet these aims;
- Improve conditions for farmland wildlife – including birds, mammals, butterflies and bees;
- Maintain and enhance landscape character – by helping to maintain important features such as traditional field boundaries [see fig. 20];
- Protect the historic environment – including archaeological features and artefacts.

(DEFRA 2005, 1.1.2)

Fig. 137.   The deserted medieval and later settlement site of Kerraton, Rattery (see also figs 13, 15 & 16), now marked by a few heaps of rubble and some scrubby trees. Like the vast majority of deserted medieval and post-medieval settlements in Devon – preliminary research by the author suggests well over 2,000 of them could be identified using old OS maps alone – this archaeological site enjoys no legal protection. Two buildings survived to second-floor height here until recent years, when they were bulldozed. Had they been included in one of DEFRA's new Stewardship Schemes, they might have survived (see also fig. 108). Photo: Sam Turner, July 2006.

Farmers participating in the scheme choose from a range of permitted management options and make a formal agreement with Natural England. They are then paid a standard sum per hectare per annum (currently £30 in the ELS). Whilst the ELS is open to all farmers, the HLS is targeted at specific regions and demands a higher level of stewardship. Applications to the Higher Level scheme are judged against various criteria set by DEFRA and their advisors, and for all areas of Devon these include the protection and enhancement of the historic landscape ('targeting statements' are published by DEFRA; for an example see RDA 2005). Applicants to the HLS can use the HLC to help understand the historic landscape of a particular area, and the scheme's administrators use it to help assess whether Stewardship is meeting its stated aims (DEFRA 2006; fig. 137).

HLC is also used to help guide tree planting and forestry schemes. The guidance notes for the English Woodland Grant Scheme administered by the Forestry Commission state that existing and new woodland should enhance the landscape and that woodland management should take the cultural and historic character of the surrounding countryside into consideration (Forestry Commission 2007). Applicants for programmes such as Woodland Management Grants must seek advice from local historic environment officers. In such cases the HLC can be consulted to show whether woodland once existed in a particular area, or whether woodland is characteristic of locations similar to a proposed site. In Devon and Cornwall, for example, woodland is commonly found on lower, steeper valley sides. These areas have often been subject to post-medieval clearance, and it might be considered appropriate to plant trees in them once more. The HLC shows that woods were rarely found in most areas on hilltops or within medieval field systems: avoiding tree planting in such places might best enhance the traditional character of the landscape (see e.g. DNPA 2005: 25).

Planning

HLC data is routinely being used by county council Historic Environment Services to inform development control and other planning work. In combination with other elements of Historic Environment Records – for example databases of archaeological sites and monuments, historic OS maps and air photographs – HLCs can help council officers in historic environment and planning departments to better understand the context and impact of proposed developments. In the last few years the HLC has been used in Devon to inform responses to major planning applications including power stations, new towns, industrial developments, airport expansion, pipelines and roads. The value of HLC in such contexts is increasingly being realised by other agencies beyond heritage organisations and county councils. For example, in 2006 the UK's Highways Agency drew up new guidelines on how to take the historic character of the landscape into account when new road schemes are being planned. Instead of simple one-size-fits-all solutions, the document stipulates that the impact of each new road on historic landscape character should henceforth be assessed at a local scale using HLC, in addition to the existing archaeological and historic buildings assessments. Importantly, the document also outlines a range of significant measures that can be taken to mitigate disruption and damage to landscape character, from landscaping and boundary restoration to changing the proposed route of new roads (Highways Agency 2006).

HLC AND THE FUTURE

Where successful, the current applications of HLC will continue to be used and developed by regional historic environment services. Increasingly, HLC may have a wider role to play in facilitating debate and interaction between different groups with interests in the landscape (fig. 138).

In these respects, HLC could play a useful role in fulfilling the obligations relating to landscape enshrined in the European Landscape Convention. The Convention was signed by the UK government in 2006 and has now come into force. According to the broad but concise definition it proposes, landscape is:

> an area, as perceived by people, whose character is the result of the action and interaction of natural and/or human factors (Council of Europe 2000: Article 1).

HLC was developed at much the same time as the European Landscape Convention, and the two share many concerns. Like HLC, the ELC does not promote certain places as more important than others in an absolute sense. In particular, both emphasise the ubiquity of landscape: it is urban as well as rural, 'everyday' and ordinary as well as special or outstanding, and not only well-preserved and formally designated but also 'degraded' or damaged. The ELC is a forward-looking Convention, and is concerned with how people will create and shape their landscapes in the future (Council of Europe 2002: 5-6). 'Landscape protection' is only one of the three instruments the ELC proposes for looking after landscape: both landscape management (upkeep focussed on continuing and modifying the *processes* of landscape creation) and landscape planning (including enhancement,

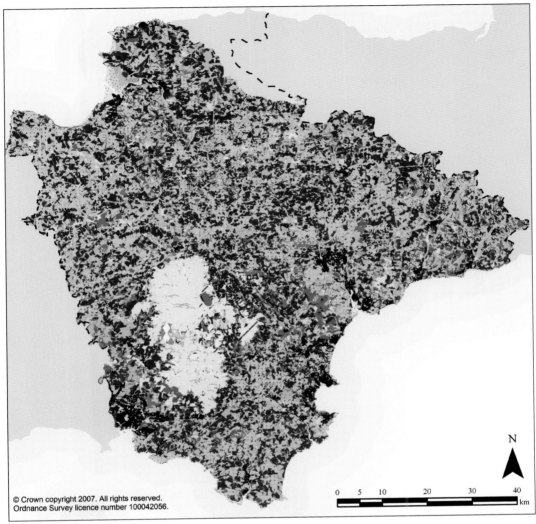

N

0   5   10   20   30   40
km

Fig. 138.   The historic landscape character of Devon, *c.* 2000. Source: Devon HLC.

change and creation) are seen to play bigger roles (Sarlöv Herlin 2004; Selman 2006). Both management and planning need access to knowledge and ideas about why the landscape today looks and feels as it does. It is important that landscape archaeology becomes one of the disciplines helping to inform and guide the formation of landscapes for the future, and HLC could provide an appropriate mechanism for doing so.

New planning legislation in the UK has been moving in a similar direction, with more emphasis on both public participation and the recognition of value in ordinary landscapes. Over the last ten years, county councils and local authorities have been using the perspectives of HLC more and more to help inform their planning policies. Until 2004, development strategies for each county were expressed as County Structure Plans and Local Plans (combined as Unitary Development Plans in metropolitan areas), with Regional

Fig. 139.   Walking up a Devon lane in summer. Photo: Sam Turner, July 2006.

Planning Guidance providing local interpretations of statutory planning. HLCs had begun to influence all these through formal Landscape Assessments and Strategies (Clark *et al.* 2004, ch. 2 & 3). However, the 2004 Town Planning and Compulsory Purchase Act abolished this framework and replaced it with Local Development Frameworks (LDFs) prepared by local authorities and Regional Spatial Strategies (RSSs) prepared by regional assemblies. Overall the new emphasis focuses more on spatial issues such as maintaining landscape character, so initiatives like HLC should have an important and direct role to play in informing future priorities (Garrod & Whitby 2005: 219-22). For example, the draft South West Regional Spatial Strategy specifically mentions characterisation as an appropriate way to inform our understanding of the landscape and provide sensitive options for future management (SWRA 2006: 149).

Like the European Landscape Convention, which emphasises the value of landscape to people, Local Development Frameworks put much more emphasis than their predecessors on public participation in the planning process. Local authorities are required to document this participation in the 'Statement of Community Involvement' they must prepare as part of the LDF (e.g. DNPA 2007). One way authorities might facilitate public participation on landscape issues is through HLC. As I suggested in Chapter 2, an 'archaeological' approach like HLC could be used to bring together different people's perspectives on particular landscapes because it allows debate to be framed effectively in reference to the same physical features (see also Turner 2006b). The emphasis laid by the new planning regime on both character-based approaches and community involvement should provide an excellent opportunity for those working with the historic environment to establish links between different disciplines and the wider public. If we can develop fair means to include a real range of interested people, HLC and related approaches could prove ways to open up debate and discussion from many different angles. As described in this book, HLC is largely concerned with the historic aspects of landscape character. But if we can encourage people to value the historicity of the landscape as a valuable resource, it will not necessarily mean other interests are damaged. Instead, it might help foster more balanced and wider-ranging discussions about what we really value and how we should best look after our landscapes in the future (fig. 139).

BIBLIOGRAPHY

Aldred, O., 2001. *Somerset & Exmoor National Park Historic Landscape Characterisation Project,1999–2000,* unpublished report (2 vols.), Taunton: Somerset County Council.

Allan, J., 1994. 'Medieval pottery and the dating of deserted settlements on Dartmoor', *Devon Archaeological Society Proceedings* 52, 141-8.

Alcock, N., 1975. 'Fields and farms in an east Devon parish', *Transactions of the Devonshire Association* 107, 93-172.

Altenberg, K., 2003. *Experiencing Landscapes: a Study of Space and Identity in Three Marginal Areas of Medieval Britain and Scandinavia,* Lund Studies in Medieval Archaeology 31, Stockholm: Almqvist & Wiksell International.

Austin, D., R. Daggett & M. Walker, 1980. 'Farms and fields in Okehampton park, Devon: the problems of studying medieval landscape', *Landscape History* 2, 39-57.

Austin, D., G. Gerrard & T. Greeves, 1989. 'Tin and agriculture in the middle ages and beyond: landscape archaeology in St Neot parish, Cornwall', *Cornish Archaeology* 28, 5-251.

Barnes, G. & T. Williamson, 2006. *Hedgerow History: Ecology, History and Landscape Character*, Macclesfield: Windgather Press.

Barrett, J., 1994. *Fragments from Antiquity. An Archaeology of Social Life in Britain, 2900-1200 BC*, Oxford: Blackwell.

Beacham, P., 1990. 'The longhouse' in P. Beacham (ed.), *Devon Building*, Tiverton: Devon Books, 47-59.

Bettey, J., 1999. 'The development of watermeadows in the southern counties' in H. Cook & T. Williamson (eds), *Water Management in the English Landscape,* Edinburgh: Edinburgh University Press, 179-195.

Boldon, D., 1988. 'Roadford reservoir: a hedgerow survey', *Nature in Devon* 9, 53-64.

Bonney, D., 1971. 'Former farms and fields at Challacombe, Manaton, Dartmoor' in K. Gregory & W. Ravenhill (eds), *Exeter Essays in Geography in Honour of Arthur Davies,* Exeter: University of Exeter, 83-91.

Booker, F., 1967. *The Industrial Archaeology of the Tamar Valley*, Newton Abbot: David and Charles.

Booker, F., 1970. 'Industry' in C. Gill (ed.), *Dartmoor: a New Study*, Newton Abbot: David & Charles, 100-138.

Brandon, P., 1979. 'Appendix: the medieval fields', 150-152 in G. Beresford, 'Three deserted medieval settlements on Dartmoor: a report on the late E. Marie Minter's excavations' *Medieval Archaeology* 23, 98-158.

Brian, A., 1999. 'The allocation of strips in Lammas Meadows by the casting of lots', *Landscape History* 21, 43-58.

Bull, E., 1998. 'Cornwall's historic field boundaries: a review', unpublished report for Cornwall Archaeological Unit, Truro: CAU.

Cannell, J., 2005. *The Archaeology of Woodland Exploitation in the Greater Exmoor Area in the Historic Period*, BAR British Series 398, Oxford: British Archaeological Reports.

Carew, R., 1953. *The Survey of Cornwall*, (ed. F. Halliday), London: Andrew Melrose.

Caseldine, C., 1999. 'Environmental setting' in R. Kain & W. Ravenhill (eds), *Historical Atlas of South-West England*, Exeter: University of Exeter Press, 25-34.

C.C.C., 1994. 'Cornwall HLC 'types' maps', unpublished HLC maps, Cornwall Archaeological Unit, Truro: Cornwall County Council.

C.C.C., 1996. *Cornwall Landscape Assessment 1994*, Truro: Cornwall County Council.

C.H.E.S., 2001. 'Round-up for 2000-2001', *Archaeology Alive/Hendhyskans yn Fyw* 9, 20.

Child, P., 1990. 'Farmhouse building traditions' in P. Beacham (ed.), *Devon Building*, Tiverton: Devon Books, 33-46.

Child, S., 2001. 'Devon fields enclosed and regretted: a seventeenth century argument among north Devon farmers', *The Devon Historian*, 62, 22-25.

Clare, T. & R. Bunce, 2006. 'The potential for using trees to help define historic landscape character zones: a case study in the English Lake District', *Landscape and Urban Planning* 74, 34-45.

Clark, J., J. Darlington, & G. Fairclough, 2004. *Using Historic Landscape Characterisation*, London: English Heritage/Lancashire County Council.

Chouquer, G., 1993. *Entre Bourgogne et Franche-Comté: Histoire d'un Paysage de l'Époque Gauloise à nos Jours*, Paris: Editions Errance.

Common Ground, 2000. *The Common Ground Book of Orchards: Conservation, Culture and Community*, London: Common Ground.

Costen, M., 1994. 'Settlement in Wessex in the tenth century: the charter evidence' in M. Aston & C. Lewis (eds), *The Medieval Landscape of Wessex*, Oxford: Oxbow Books, 97-113.

Council of Europe, 2000. *European Landscape Convention*. Florence: Council of Europe (European Treaty Series No. 176). http://conventions.coe.int/Treaty/en/Treaties/Html/176.htm (Consulted 12th July 2006).

Council of Europe, 2002. *The European Landscape Convention*. (= Naturopa Issue 98 / 2002). Strasbourg: Council of Europe. http://www.coe.int/T/E/Cultural_Co-operation/Environment/Resources/Naturopa_Magazine/index.asp (Consulted 17th July 2006).

Countryside Commission, 1994. *The Landscape of Bodmin Moor*, Cheltenham: Countryside Commission.

Cousins, S., 2004. 'Why hedge dating doesn't work', *Landscape History* 26, 77-85.

Crawford, O., 1953. *Archaeology in the Field*, London: Phoenix House.

Crumley, C., 1999. 'Sacred landscapes: constructed and conceptualised' in W. Ashmore & B. Knapp (eds.), *Archaeologies of Landscape: Contemporary Perspectives*, Oxford: Blackwell, 269-276.

Currie, C., 2003. 'Dartington Hall and Shilston Barton: archaeological excavations at two Devon gardens, 1991–2000' in R. Wilson-North (ed.), *The Lie of the Land: Aspects of the Archaeology and History of the Designed Landscape in the South West of England*, Exeter: Mint Press, 51-65.

Darvill, T., C. Gerrard & B. Startin. 1993. 'Identifying and protecting historic landscapes', *Antiquity* 67, 563-574.

D.C.C., 2005. 'Species-rich hedges' in *Devon Biodiversity Action Plan*, Exeter: Devon County Council. Available: http://www.devon.gov.uk/dbap-land-species.pdf (last consulted 7th March 2007).

D.E.F.R.A., 2005. *Entry Level Stewardship Handbook*. Available: http://www.defra.gov.uk/erdp/schemes/els/handbook/ (last consulted 3rd March 2007).

D.E.F.R.A., 2006. *Environmental Stewardship Evaluation Plan*. Available: http://www.defra.gov.uk/erdp/pdfs/es/ES-EvaluationPlan-Feb06.pdf (last consulted 3rd March 2007).

D.N.P.A., 2002. *Houndtor: Deserted Medieval Settlement*, Bovey Tracey: Dartmoor National Park Authority.

D.N.P.A., 2004. *The Okehampton Bypass: a Case Study in Decision Making*, Bovey Tracey: Dartmoor National Park Authority. Available: http://www.dartmoor-npa.gov.uk/print/lab-okebypass.pdf (last consulted 1st March 2007).

D.N.P.A., 2005. *A Woodland Strategy for Dartmoor National Park, 2005–2010*, Bovey Tracey: Dartmoor National Park Authority. Available: http://www.dartmoor-npa.gov.uk/index/lookingafter/laf-naturalenv/laf-treeswoodlands/laf-woodlandsstrategy.htm (last consulted 4th March 2007).

D.N.P.A., 2007. *Dartmoor Local Development Framework – Sstatement of Community Involvement*, Bovey Tracey: Dartmoor National Park Authority. Available: http://www.dartmoor-npa.gov.uk/index/planning/pl-forwardplanning/pl-localdevframework/pl-comminvolve.htm (last consulted 4th March 2007).

Dommelen, P. van, 1999. 'Exploring everyday places and cosmologies' in W. Ashmore & B. Knapp (eds.), *Archaeologies of Landscape: Contemporary Perspectives,* Oxford: Blackwell, 277-285.

Dyer, C., 1997. 'Peasants and farmers: rural settlements and landscapes in an age of transition' in D. Gaimster & P. Stamper (eds), *The Age of Transition: the Archaeology of English Culture 1400-1600*, Oxford: Oxbow, 61-76.

Dymond, R., 1856. 'Devonshire fields and hedges', *Journal of the Bath and West of England Society* 4, 132-148.

English Nature, 2006. 'Ancient Woodland Inventory (Provisional) for England – Digital Boundaries', London: Natural England. Available: http://www.english-nature.org.uk/pubs/gis/tech_aw.htm (last consulted 27th February 2007).

Fairclough, G., 2002. 'Cultural landscape, computers and characterization' in G. Burenhult (ed.), *Archaeological Informatics: Pushing the Envelope*, Proceedings of the 29th CAA Conference, Gotland, April 2001. BAR International Series 1016. Oxford: Archaeopress, 277-294.

Fairclough, G., 2003. "The Long Chain': archaeology, historical landscape characterization and time depth in the landscape', in H. Palang & G. Fry (eds), *Landscape Interfaces: Cultural Heritage in Changing Landscapes*, Dordrecht: Kluwer Academic Publishers, 295-318.

Fairclough, G. & L. Macinnes, 2003. *Understanding Historic Landscape Character*, Topic Paper 5. Landscape Character Assessment Guidance for England and Scotland. Countryside Agency, Scottish Natural Heritage, Historic Scotland & English Heritage. Available: http://www.ccnetwork.org.uk/lca_topic_5_sum.htm, (last consulted 17th July 2006).

Fairclough, G. & A. Wigley, 2005. 'Historic landscape characterisation: an English approach to landscape understanding and the management of change' in M. Ruiz del Árbol & A. Orejas (eds), *Landscapes as Cultural Heritage in the European Research*, Madrid: CSIC, 87-106.

Fairclough, G., G. Lambrick & A. McNab (eds.), 1999. *Yesterday's World, Tomorrow's Landscape: the English Heritage Landscape Project 1992–94,* London: English Heritage.

Finberg, H., 1949. 'The open field in Devonshire', *Antiquity* 23, 180-187.

Finberg, H., 1951. *Tavistock Abbey. A Study in the Social and Economic History of Devon*, Cambridge: Cambridge University Press.

Finberg, H., 1953. *The Early Charters of Devon and Cornwall*, Leicester: University College of Leicester.

Finberg, H., 1969. 'The open field in Devon' in H. Finberg, *West Country Historical Studies*, Newton Abbot: David and Charles, 129-151.

Finberg, H., 1971. 'Ayshford and Boehill', *Transactions of the Devonshire Association* 103, 19-24.

Finneran, N. & S. Turner, 2003. 'An archaeological history of the landscape of Little Haldon, Teignmouth, south Devon', *Transactions of the Devonshire Association* 135, 235-259.

Fitzherbert, 1523. *The Boke of Surveying and Improvements,* London, reprinted Amsterdam, 1974: Theatrum Orbis Terrarum.

Fitzpatrick, A., C. Butterworth & J. Grove, 1999. *Prehistoric and Roman Sites in East Devon: the A30 Honiton to Exeter Improvement DBFO, 1996-9*, Salisbury: Wessex Archaeology Report 16.

Fleming, A., 1988. *The Dartmoor Reaves*, London: Batsford.

Fleming, A., 1994a. 'The reaves reviewed', *Devon Archaeological Society Proceedings* 52, 63-74.

Fleming, A., 1994b. 'Medieval and post-medieval cultivation on Dartmoor: a landscape archaeologist's view', *Devon Archaeological Society Proceedings* 52, 101-117

Fleming, A. & N. Ralph, 1982. 'Medieval settlement and land use on Holne Moor, Dartmoor: the landscape evidence' *Medieval Archaeology* 26, 101-137.

Fletcher, M. & C. Dunn, 1999. 'The evolution and changing perceptions of a moorland landscape', in P. Pattison, D. Field and S. Ainsworth (eds), *Patterns of the Past: Essays in Landscape Archaeology for Christopher Taylor*, Oxford: Oxbow Books, 129-134.

Foard, G., D. Hall & T. Partida, 2005. 'Rockingham Forest, Northamptonshire: the evolution of a landscape', *Landscapes* 6.2, 1-29.

Forestry Commission, 2007. *English Woodland Grant Scheme.* Available: http://www.forestry.gov.uk/forestry/infd-6dccen (last consulted 3rd March 2007).

Fox, C., 1938. *The Personality of Britain: its Influence on Inhabitant and Invader in Prehistoric and Early Historic Times*, 3rd edn, Cardiff: National Museum of Wales.

Fox, H., 1971. 'A Geographical Study of the Field Systems of Devon and Cornwall', unpublished Ph.D thesis, University of Cambridge.

Fox, H., 1972. 'Field systems of east and south Devon. Part 1: east Devon', *Transactions of the Devonshire Association* 104, 81-135.

Fox, H., 1973. 'Outfield cultivation in Devon and Cornwall: a reinterpretation' in M. Havinden (ed.), *Husbandry and Marketing in the South West, 1500-1800*, Exeter: Exeter Papers in Economic History 8, 19-38.

Fox, H., 1975. 'The chronology of enclosure and economic development in medieval Devon', *Economic History Review* n.s. 28 (2), 181-202.

Fox, H., 1983. 'Contraction: Desertion and Dwindling of Dispersed Settlement in a Devon Parish', *31st Annual Report of the Medieval Village Research Group*, 40-42.

Fox, H., 1989. 'Peasant farmers, patterns of settlement and *pays*: transformations in the landscapes of Devon and Cornwall during the later middle ages' in R. Higham (ed.), *Landscape and Townscape in the South West*, Exeter: University of Exeter Press, 41-73.

Fox, H., 1991a. 'The occupation of the land: Devon and Cornwall' in E. Miller (ed.), *The Agrarian History of England and Wales, Vol. III, 1348–1500*, Cambridge: Cambridge University Press, 152-74.

Fox, H., 1991b. 'Farming practice and techniques: Devon and Cornwall' in E. Miller (ed.), *The Agrarian History of England and Wales, Vol. III, 1348–1500*, Cambridge: Cambridge University Press, 303-323.

Fox, H., 1994. 'Medieval Dartmoor as seen through its account rolls', *Devon Archaeological Society Proceedings* 52, 141-179.

Fox, H., 1995. 'Servants, cottagers and tied cottages during the later Middle Ages: towards a regional dimension', *Rural History* 6(2), 125-154.

Fox, H., 2005. 'Fragmented manors and the customs of the Anglo-Saxons' in S. Keynes & A. Smith, *Anglo-Saxons: Studies Presented to Cyril Roy Hart*, Dublin: Four Courts Press, 78-97.

Fox, H., forthcoming. *Alluring Uplands: Transhumance and Pastoral Management on Dartmoor, 950-1550.*

Fox, H. & O. Padel, 1998. *Cornish Lands of the Arundells of Lanherne, Fourteenth to Sixteenth Centuries*, Devon and Cornwall Record Society (new series) 41, Exeter: D&CRS.

Franklin, L., 2006. 'Imagined landscapes: the role of archaeology, perception and folklore in the study of medieval Devon' in S. Turner (ed.), *Medieval Devon and Cornwall: Shaping an Ancient Countryside*, Macclesfield: Windgather Press, 144-161.

Fyfe, R., Brown, A. & S. Rippon, 2003. 'Mid- to late-Holocene vegetation history of Greater Exmoor, UK: estimating the spatial extent of human-induced vegetation change,' *Vegetation History and Archaeobotany* 12, 215-32.

Fyfe, R., 2006. 'Palaeoenvironmental perspectives on medieval landscape development' in S. Turner (ed.), *Medieval Devon and Cornwall: Shaping an Ancient Countryside*, Macclesfield: Windgather Press, 10-23.

Gallant, L., N. Luxton & M. Collman, 1985. 'Ancient fields on the south Devon limestone plateau', *Devon Archaeological Society Proceedings* 43, 23-37.

Gamble, C., 2001. *Archaeology: the Basics,* London: Routledge.

Garrod, G. & M. Whitby, 2006. *Strategic Countryside Management*, Oxford: Elsevier.

Gent, T. & H. Quinnell, 1999. 'Salvage recording on the Neolithic site at Haldon Belvedere', *Devon Archaeological Society Proceedings* 57, 77-104.

Gernigon, C., 2002. 'Evolution d'un paysage arboré sur la commune de Saint-Yrieix-la-Perche (87): étude du parcellaire d'une section communale de 1826 à 2000', *Travaux d'Archéologie Limousine* 22, 135-145.

Gerrard, S., 1994. 'The Dartmoor tin industry: an archaeological perspective', *Devon Archaeological Society Proceedings* 52, 173-198.

Gerrard, S., 1997. *Dartmoor*, London: English Heritage/Batsford.

Gerrard, S., 2000. *The Early British Tin Industry*, Stroud: Tempus.

Gilg, A., 1999. 'Agriculture, forestry and landscape conservation in the twentieth century', in R. Kain & W. Ravenhill (eds), *Historical Atlas of South-West England,* Exeter: University of Exeter Press, 307-321.

Gillard, M., 2002. 'The medieval landscape of the Exmoor region: enclosure and settlement in an upland fringe', unpublished PhD thesis, University of Exeter.

Given, M., A. Knapp, N. Meyer, T. Gregory, V. Kassianidou, J. Noller, L. Wells, N. Urwin, & H. Wright, 1999. 'The Sydney Cyprus Survey Project: an interdisciplinary investigation of long-term change in the north central Troodos, Cyprus', *Journal of Field Archaeology* 26, 19-39.

Grant, J., 1845. 'A few remarks on the large hedges and small enclosures of Devonshire and the adjoining counties', *Journal of the Royal Agricultural Society* 5.2, 420-429.

Gray, H., 1915. *English Field Systems*, Cambridge, Mass: Harvard University Press.

Gray, T., 2003. *Lost Devon: Creation, Change and Destruction over 500 Years*, Exeter: Mint Press.

Griffith, F., 1988. *Devon's Past: an Aerial View*, Exeter: Devon Books.

Hall, D., 1982. *Medieval Fields*, Princes Risborough: Shire Books.

Hall, M., 2006. 'Identity, memory and countermemory: the archaeology of an urban landscape', *Journal of Material Culture* 11(1/2), 189-209.

Havinden, M. & R. Stanes, 1999. 'Agriculture and rural settlement 1500–1800' in R. Kain & W. Ravenhill (eds), *Historical Atlas of South-West England,* Exeter: University of Exeter Press, 281-93.

Havinden, M. & F. Wilkinson, 1970. 'Farming' in C. Gill (ed.), *Dartmoor: a New Study*, Newton Abbot: David and Charles, 139-181.

Henderson, C. & P. Weddell, 1994. 'Medieval settlements on Dartmoor and in west Devon: the evidence from excavations', *Proceedings of the Devon Archaeological Society* 52, 119-140.

Herring, P. 1986, 'An exercise in landscape history. Pre-Norman and medieval Brown Willy and Bodmin Moor, Cornwall', unpublished MPhil thesis, 3 vols, University of Sheffield.

Herring, P., 1993. 'Examining a Romano-British boundary at Foage, Zennor', *Cornish Archaeology* 32, 17-28.

Herring, P. 1998. *Cornwall's Historic Landscape: Presenting a Method of Historic Landscape Character Assessment,* Truro: Cornwall Archaeological Unit.

Herring, P., 1999. 'Cornwall: how the historic landscape characterisation methodology was developed' in G. Fairclough (ed.), *Historic Landscape Characterisation: the 'State of the Art'*, London: English Heritage, 15-32.

Herring, P., 2004. 'Cornish uplands: medieval, post-medieval and modern extents' in I. Whyte and A. Winchester (eds), *Society, Landscape and Environment in Upland Britain,* Birmingham: Society for Landscape Studies, 37-50.

Herring, P., 2006a. 'Cornish strip fields' in S. Turner (ed.), *Medieval Devon and Cornwall. Shaping an Ancient Countryside*, Macclesfield: Windgather Press, 44-77.

Herring, P., 2006b. 'Medieval fields at Brown Willy, Bodmin Moor' in S. Turner (ed.), *Medieval Devon and Cornwall. Shaping an Ancient Countryside*, Macclesfield: Windgather Press, 78-103.

Herring, P. & D. Hooke, 1993. 'Interrogating Anglo-Saxons in St Dennis', *Cornish Archaeology* 32, 67-75.

Highways Agency, 2006. *Assessing the Effect of Road Schemes on Historic Landscape Character*, Bristol: Highways Agency.

Hooke, D., 1994. *Pre-Conquest Charter-Bounds of Devon and Cornwall*, Woodbridge: Boydell.

Hoskins, W., 1954. *Devon*, London: Collins.

Hoskins, W., 1955. *The Making of the English Landscape*, London: Hodder and Stoughton.

Hoskins, W., 1963. *Provincial England: Essays in Social and Economic History*, Lonson: Macmillan.

Hoskins, W., 1966. 'Some old Devon bartons' in W. Hoskins, *Old Devon*, London: Pan Books, 30-44.

Humphreys, C., 2004. 'Charlestown Barton, Charles, Devon', unpublished report held by Devon Historic Environment Record, Devon County Council Archaeology Service, Exeter.

Iles, R., 1994. 'The medieval, Tudor and Stuart parks of Devon' in S. Pugsley, *Devon Gardens: an Historical Survey,* (Stroud: Sutton), 21-27.

Johnson, M., 2005. 'Thinking about landscape' in C. Renfrew & P. Bahn (eds), *Archaeology: the Key Concepts*, London: Routledge, 156-159.

Jones, R. & M. Page, 2006. *Medieval Villages in an English Landscape: Beginnings and Ends*, Macclesfield: Windgather.

Kirby, K. & E. Goldberg, 2002-3. *Ancient Woodland: Guidance Material for Local Authorities*, Peterborough: English Nature. Available: http://www.english-nature.org.uk/pubs/publication/pdf/AwoodlandGuidance.pdf, (last consulted 11th August 2006).

Knapp, B. & W. Ashmore, 1999. 'Archaeological landscapes: constructed, conceptualized, ideational' in W. Ashmore & B. Knapp (eds), *Archaeologies of Landscape: Contemporary Perspectives,* Oxford: Blackwell, 1-30.

Long, W., 1935. 'Size of fields in Devon', *Farm Economist* 1.11, 224-225.

Maitland, F., 1897. *Domesday Book and Beyond*, Cambridge: Cambridge University Press.

Marshall, W., 1796a. *The Rural Economy of the West of England, Vol. 1*, London (reprinted 1970, Newton Abbot: David and Charles).

Marshall, W., 1796b. *The Rural Economy of the West of England, Vol. 2*, London (reprinted 1970, Newton Abbot: David and Charles).

McNab, A. & G. Lambrick, 1999. 'Conclusions and recommendations' in G. Fairclough, G. Lambrick & A. McNab (eds), *Yesterday's World, Tomorrow's Landscape: the English Heritage Landscape Project 1992-94*, London: English Heritage, 54-59.

Michelmore, A. & M. Proctor, 1994. 'The hedges of Farley Farm, Chudleigh', *Transactions of the Devonshire Association* 126, 57-84.

Muir, R. & N. Muir, 1987. *Hedgerows: their History and Wildlife*, London: Michael Joseph.

Newman, P., 1994. 'Tinners and tenants on south-west Dartmoor: a case-study in landscape history', *Transactions of the Devonshire Association* 126, 199-238.

Newman, P., 2003. *Deckler's Cliff Field System, East Portlemouth, Devon,* Archaeological Investigation Report Series AI/16/2003, Swindon: English Heritage.

Newman, P., 2006. 'Tin-working and the landscape of medieval Devon *c.*1150–1700' in S. Turner (ed.), *Medieval Devon and Cornwall: Shaping an Ancient Countryside*, Macclesfield: Windgather Press, 123-143.

Olwig, K., 2004. "'This is not a landscape': circulating reference and land shaping', in H. Palang, H. Sooväli, M. Antrop & G. Setten (eds), *European Rural Landscapes: Persistence and Change in a Globalising Environment*, Dordrecht: Kluwer Academic Publishers, 41-65.

Orwin, C., R. Sellick & V. Bonham-Carter, 1997. *The Reclamation of Exmoor Forest*, Tiverton: Exmoor Books.

Overton, M., 2006. 'Farming, fishing and rural settlements' in R. Kain (ed.), *The South West*, London: English Heritage, 109-130.

Padel, O., 1985. *Cornish Place-Name Elements*, Nottingham: English Place-Name Society.

Pattison, P., 1999. 'Challacombe revisited' in P. Pattison, D. Field & S. Ainsworth (eds), *Patterns of the Past: Essays in Landscape Archaeology for Christopher Taylor*, Oxford: Oxbow Books, 61-70.

Phear, J., 1889. 'Notes on Braunton Great Field', *Transactions of the Devonshire Association* 21, 202.

Pugsley, S., 1994. *Devon Gardens: an Historical Survey*, Stroud: Sutton.

Rackham, O., 1986. *The History of the Countryside*, London: Dent.

Rackham, O., 2003. *Ancient Woodland*, 2nd edition, Dalbeattie: Castlepoint Press.

R.D.A., 2005. JCA 148: *Devon Redlands*, Environmental Stewardship Targeting Statement 2005. Available: http://www.defra.gov.uk/erdp/pdfs/jca-ts/148.pdf (last consulted 3rd March 2007).

Reed, S., G. Juleff & S. Turton, 2006. 'Three late-Saxon iron smelting furnaces at Burlescombe, Devon', *Devon Archaeological Society Proceedings* 64, 71-122.

Riley, H. & R. Wilson-North, 2001. *The Field Archaeology of Exmoor*, London: English Heritage.

Rippon, S., 1996. *Gwent Levels: the Evolution of a Wetland Landscape*, CBA Research Report 105, York: Council for British Archaeology.

Rippon, S., 2000. *The Transformation of Coastal Wetlands: Exploitation and Management of Marshland Landscapes in North West Europe during the Roman and Medieval Periods*, Oxford: British Academy/Oxford University Press.

Robbins, K., A. Butler, M. Turner & M. Lobley, 2006. 'Agricultural change and farm incomes in Devon: an update'. Available: http://www.devon.gov.uk/agricultural_change_and_ farm_incomes_in_devon.pdf (last consulted 3rd March 2007).

Roberts, B. & S. Wrathmell, 2000. *An Atlas of Rural Settlement in England*, London: English Heritage.

Roberts, B. & S. Wrathmell, 2002. *Region and Place*, London: English Heritage.

Roymans, N., 1995. 'The cultural biography of urnfields and the long-term history of a mythical landscape', *Archaeological Dialogues* 2(1), 2-24.

Sarlöv Herlin, I., 2004. 'New challenges in the field of spatial planning: landscapes', *Landscape Research* 29(4), 399-411.

Sawyer, P., 1968. *Anglo-Saxon Charters. An Annotated Handlist and Bibliography*, London: Royal Historical Society.

S.C.C. n.d. *Somerset Historic Environment Record*, Taunton: Somerset County Council.

Available: http://webapp1.somerset.gov.uk/her/sop.asp?flash=true (last consulted 15th March 2007).

Selman, P., 2006. *Planning at Landscape Scale*, London: Routledge.

Sitelines, n.d. *Sitelines: the Tyne and Wear Historic Environment Record*, Newcastle: Tyne and Wear Museums. Available: http://sine7.ncl.ac.uk/sl/home.htm (last consulted 15th March 2007).

Smith, K., J. Coppen, G. Wainwright & S. Becket, 1981. 'The Shaugh Moor project: third report – settlement and environmental investigations', *Proceedings of the Prehistoric Society* 47, 205-273.

Somers Cocks, J., 1970. 'Exploitation' in C. Gill (ed.), *Dartmoor: a New Study*, Newton Abbot: David and Charles, 245-275.

S.W.R.A., 2006. *Draft Regional Spatial Strategy for the South West, 2006–2026*, Taunton: South West Regional Assembly. Available: http://www.southwest-ra.gov.uk/nqcontent.cfm?a_id=538 (last consulted 4th March 2007).

Tamar AONB & Cornwall County Council, 2002. 'Tamar Valley fruit growing and market gardening: outline management plan', unpublished report, Truro: Historic Environment Service, Cornwall County Council/Tamar Valley AONB Service.

Taylor, C., 2002. 'Nucleated settlement: a view from the frontier', *Landscape History* 24, 53-71.

Thirsk, J., 1967. 'The farming regions of England' in J. Thirsk (ed.), *The Agrarian History of England and Wales, Vol. 5, 1500-1640*, Cambridge: Cambridge University Press, 1-112.

Thirsk, J., 1987. *England's Agricultural Regions and Agrarian History, 1500–1750*, London: Macmillan Education.

Thomas, C., 1994. *And Shall These Mute Stones Speak?*, Cardiff: University of Wales Press.

Thorn, C. & F. Thorn (eds), 1985. *Domesday Book 9: Devon*, 2 vols, Chichester: Phillimore.

Thorndycraft, V., D. Pirrie & A. Brown, 2004. 'Alluvial records of medieval and prehistoric tin mining on Dartmoor, south-west England', *Geoarchaeology* 19(3), 219-236.

Thorpe, J., & J. Cox, 1994. 'The traditional Dartmoor farmstead; the end', *Devon Archaeological Society Proceedings* 52, 241-269.

Turner, S., 2004. 'The changing ancient landscape: south-west England, *c.*1700-1900', *Landscapes* 5(1), 18-34.

Turner, S., 2005. 'Devon Historic Landscape Characterisation: Phase 1 Report, January 2005', Exeter: Devon County Council. Available: http://www.devon.gov.uk/index/environment/historic_environment/landscapes/landscape-characterisation.htm (last consulted 28th June 2007).

Turner, S., 2006a. *Making a Christian Landscape: the Countryside in Early Medieval Cornwall, Devon and Wessex*, Exeter: University of Exeter Press.

Turner, S., 2006b. 'Historic landscape characterisation: a landscape archaeology for research, management and planning', *Landscape Research* 31, 385-398.

Turner, S., forthcoming (2007). 'Fields, property and agricultural innovation in late medieval and early modern south-west England' in K. Giles & J. Finch (eds), *Post-Medieval Estate Landscapes*, Leeds: Society for Post-Medieval Archaeology.

Turner, S. & G. Fairclough, forthcoming (2007). 'Common culture: the archaeology of landscape character in Europe', in D. Hicks, L. McAtackney & G. Fairclough (eds), *Envisioning Landscape: Perspectives and Politics in Archaeology and Heritage*, Walnut Creek, CA: Left Coast Press.

Vancouver, C., 1808. *General View of the Agriculture of the County of Devon*, London: R. Phillips.

Warnock, S., 2002. 'Level 1 Typology of Landscape Character: Report to Accompany the Creation of a National (Level 1) Landscape Description Unit Framework for the Countryside Agency', unpublished report, Living Landscapes Project, Dept of Geography, University of Reading.

Waterhouse, R., 2003. 'Garden archaeology in South Devon' in R. Wilson-North (ed.), *The Lie of the Land: Aspects of the Archaeology and History of the Designed Landscape in the South West of England*, Exeter: Mint Press, 66-82.

Webb, B., 2006. 'The environmental setting of human occupation' in R. Kain (ed.), *England's Landscape: the South West*, London: Collins/English Heritage, 15-40.

Weddell, P. & S. Reed, 1997. 'Excavations at Sourton Down, Okehampton 1986–1991: Roman road, deserted medieval hamlet and other landscape features', *Devon Archaeological Society Proceedings* 55, 39-147.

Weddell, P., S. Reed & S. Simpson, 1993. 'Excavation of the Exeter-Dorchester Roman road at the River Yarty and the Roman fort ditch and settlement site as Woodbury, near Axminster', *Devon Archaeological Society Proceedings* 51, 33-133.

Widgren, M., 2004. 'Can landscapes be read?' in H. Palang, H. Sooväli, M. Antrop & G. Setten (eds), *European Rural Landscapes: Persistence and Change in a Globalising Environment*, Dordrecht: Kluwer Academic Publishers, 455-465.

Williamson, T., 1998. 'The Scole-Dickleburgh field system revisited', *Landscape History* 20, 19-28.

Williamson, T., 2000. 'Understanding enclosure', *Landscapes* 1(1), 56-79.

Williamson, T., 2002. *The Transformation of Rural England: Farming and the Landscape 1700–1870*, Exeter: University of Exeter Press.

Williamson, T., 2003. *Shaping Medieval Landscapes*, Macclesfield: Windgather Press.

Williamson, T., 2006. 'Mapping field patterns: a case study from eastern England', *Landscapes* 7(1), 55-67.

INDEX

Italic page numbers refer to illustrations